MW00413627

The 9 Month Investment

The
9 Month
Investment

A Passive Investors Guide to Achieving 10 Years
Worth of Wealth Accumulation in Only 9 Months

Darin Garman, CCIM

Glazer-Kennedy
publishing

Imprint of Morgan James Publishing
NEW YORK

The 9 Month Investment
A Passive Investors Guide to Achieving 10 Years
Worth of Wealth Accumulation in Only 9 Months

Copyright © 2010 Darin Garman. All rights reserved.

No part of this publication may be reproduced or transmitted in any form or by any means, mechanical or electronic, including photocopying and recording, or by any information storage and retrieval system, without permission in writing from the author or publisher (except by a reviewer, who may quote brief passages and/or short brief video clips in a review.)

Disclaimer: The Publisher and the Author make no representations or warranties with respect to the accuracy or completeness of the contents of this work and specifically disclaim all warranties, including without limitation warranties of fitness for a particular purpose. No warranty may be created or extended by sales or promotional materials. The advice and strategies contained herein may not be suitable for every situation. This work is sold with the understanding that the Publisher is not engaged in rendering legal, accounting, or other professional services. If professional assistance is required, the services of a competent professional person should be sought. Neither the Publisher nor the Author shall be liable for damages arising herefrom. The fact that an organization or website is referred to in this work as a citation and/or a potential source of further information does not mean that the Author or the Publisher endorses the information the organization or website may provide or recommendations it may make. Further, readers should be aware that internet websites listed in this work may have changed or disappeared between when this work was written and when it is read.

ISBN 978-0-98237-936-3

Library of Congress Control Number: 2009943423

Published by

Glazer-Kennedy
publishing

an imprint of
Morgan James Publishing
1225 Franklin Ave., STE 325
Garden City, NY 11530-1693
Toll Free 800-485-4943
www.MorganJamesPublishing.com

Habitat
for Humanity®
Peninsula
Building Partner

In an effort to support local communities, raise awareness and funds, Morgan James Publishing donates one percent of all book sales for the life of each book to Habitat for Humanity. Get involved today, visit **www.HelpHabitatForHumanity.org.**

INTRODUCTION

"My Investment Increased Over $977,000 In 9 Months Using This System"
— Mike Miget, St. Louis, MO

Dear Fellow Investor:

Does the above REAL testimonial excite you? I sure hope so because it is a REAL testimonial from a REAL person that got involved and used the strategies you are about to read in this book to make massive gains to his net worth in a very short period of time.

One thing that you need to understand is the world of conventional thinking and investing is making a huge shift right now—it needs to. As of the writing of this book there are many people that have invested their hard earned money month after month, year after year for 20, 30 or even 40 years only to see it at a fraction of what it should be worth OR worse, have it disappear altogether.

The two fallacies with this 'accumulation' type investing are you:

1. Assume it will be there and worth more 30 years down the road.
2. Forces You To Put Off The Benefits of Wealth UNTIL You Invest For 20–40 Years. In the meantime you need to keep your nose to the grindstone and hope it all works out.

These are fallacies because there are of course no guarantees. None. Just because you thought this method of investing would work and you have been told by everyone that it would (probably since you were a kid) does NOT mean the money will be there. Also, you assume that by working hard for 30 years that entitles you to money in the end. It doesn't. Or, maybe you have recently lost or taken a big hit in your savings and you are not 18 anymore—short time to build it up. The Calvary is not coming to your aid.

What this book will allow you to do is stop taking chances that can cost you 20 years of your life and work with a proven system that will allow for REAL fast wealth accumulation. Not only that it will allow you to enjoy this TODAY and not have to wait 30 years from now.

Good luck and let me know how you come out!

Darin R. Garman, CCIM

TABLE OF CONTENTS

THE 9 MONTH INVESTMENT

A PASSIVE INVESTORS GUIDE TO ACHIEVING
10 YEARS WORTH OF WEALTH ACCUMULATION IN ONLY 9 MONTHS.

About This Book:

DON'T JUDGE A BOOK BY ITS COVER!

Dear Reader…

There is one thing that bugs me about many of the books you see—especially any financial improvement or wealth improvement books, you know, that have to do with making money or growing your wealth. They are all way too long…way too thick.

For example. I just got done reading a book on how to invest in discounted and troubled mortgages with the author probably someone that you have heard of. The book was over 400 pages with many of those pages being charts, graphs, property analysis, etc. I have no problem with the information in the book. I liked it and I thought it to be accurate. What I did not like is that the author and publisher assumes one thing that I think is a big mistake, and I see many authors making this mistake.

They assume that the person reading it has the time, the money, and the patience to make mistakes to make the information work. In other words, they assume that the person reading it is going to do it themselves. Of course whenever you do it yourself, especially the first time, nothing goes smoothly, mistakes are made, etc. You know what I mean. In my opinion, the author makes the wrong assumption about people in today's world.

Here we are and it's almost 2011 and people today have no time. You will like chapter 1 of the book, by the way, because I deal with that directly. In our fast paced fast action society people do not have time—even if they want to grow their wealth and be rich—they are very, very short on time, and if honest have very little free time on their hands.

Years ago I discovered a REAL WORLD method of achieving huge financial gains in ones net worth and cash flow that would usually take years—but with this system it can be achieved in a matter of months!

In today's world we are at an interesting crossroads. Most of us do not have enough time and when it comes to achieving our wealth goals faster, it is going to require time that we don't have. Plus, many of us wish we had MORE TIME to achieve our wealth goals. For example, many people have either started late in their accumulation of money for a comfortable retirement, OR they have had their retirement portfolios cut in half over the years because of a sagging stock market and economy. It's these folks that wish they actually had more time to achieve and accumulate wealth…not less.

This is the underpinning of this book—The 9 Month Investment. This book will essentially show you how to achieve 10 years of wealth accumulation in only 9 months. Repeated over a three year period, you can achieve the same wealth accumulation in 3 years as it takes the average person 30. No kidding.

But there are a couple of ground rules you will have to follow in order to get this going for you at the very soonest.

1. Keep an open mind. I promise you my methods work. They have worked for me and others. What I am going to reveal in this book is not conventional, so it will take unconventional thinking to not only appreciate it more but to also to get it going for you sooner vs. later.

2. Make sure you understand this will take SOME work from you. Yeah, I wish I could tell you that you can sit back in your comfy chair sipping on your favorite drink and all of this will just happen automatically. Sorry, can't do it. This WILL take some work and effort from you, okay? BUT, the good news is

that it will not take very much time vs. a new part time job or anything like that. So, it will require some work from you but it will be nothing compared to the results you will get as a result. Be prepared to make $1,000+ per hour!

I look forward to hearing of your success stories. Please contact me with them and your progress at darin_garman@msn.com

Best,

Darin Garman, CCIM
America's Apartment Specialist
743 10th St.
Marion, Iowa 52302
FAX 1-866-212-2838
Darin_Garman@msn.com

SECTION I—THE TYPE OF INVESTMENT THAT WILL FOLD TIME

PART I—THE INVESTMENT VEHICLE TO USE

CHAPTER 1

THE TIME WE HAVE PARADOX AND HOW THIS SMALL BOOK WILL MAKE YOU RICH, FASTER...

When it comes to making money, especially in terms of building your NET WORTH, cash flow and having your financial dreams realized, I hate to break it to you but, TIME is NOT on your side. You see conventional thinking would tell you that it is. There are many investment gurus, books, etc. that espouse the virtue of time and the accumulation of wealth over 20, 30 or even 50 years. Hey, there is nothing wrong with this...unless you like to wait 40 years!!

You see time is our enemy. It is the enemy of every person that wants to be better off financially. Be successful financially. Time is a killer of life, really. Think about it. Let's say your goal is to have a Five Million Dollar Net Worth. If you follow conventional wisdom and conventional investing that is indeed possible, however, how old will you be when you finally "make it?" How much will you REALLY be able to enjoy that financial success? By the way, in case you did not know it, you are NOT immortal. I mean, I want to enjoy this financial success now not when I am 93 with a very limited amount of time ahead of me, which leads me to something else.

Many of us think we are immortal. Why else would we take part in investments that take so damn long to grow? So damn long to become assets we can use? I have a few friends and many acquaintances that have worked long and hard for 30+ years and had their wealth snatched away from them by a variety of circumstances. Unexpected death, unexpected financial problems, health problems, etc. robbed these folks of their wealth AFTER 20–40 years of accumulating it. It's just not fair BUT it is the way of the world and its not your fault. You did your part didn't you? Problem is with the world today, you can do your part and still fall flat on your face. I hate it too!

But what IF you could accomplish your financial goals in just a fraction of time? What if you could be 20 years younger when you reached that Five Million Dollar Net Worth Goal and have plenty of time to enjoy it? Or, in the event you did have a financial problem you have PLENTY of time to make those lost millions back?

In a nutshell this is what this book is going to be all about. Basically eliminating time to get to your financial goals. Or as the Sci-Fi geeks say 'folding time.'

Now, don't get me wrong. This is not like The Matrix movies with Keanu Reeves and Laurence Fishbourne where we will be stopping time and magically making our days last more than 24 hours. With all of our scientific and technological breakthroughs, it can't be done... at least not YET anyway. No, what I am talking about is speeding up, making the time factor go away. In other words...

Getting Our Financial Chips NOW vs. waiting years and working our tails off to get it. Turning 'traditional investing' on its ear and getting the Net Worth we want NOW vs. waiting years and years. This is not only a HUGE breakthrough in you becoming financially successful, but it can work for you no matter where you are at in your current financial situation NOW.

This is a HUGE BREAKTHROUGH.

Think about this...

When you eliminate TIME from the equation, you can not only build wealth FASTER but you can make up for lost time! How many people want to make up for lost time, investment mistakes, a draining of their wealth over time for various reasons? I can tell you a lot.

Think how you will feel when you can make the same amount of money and add it to your net worth in a period of 9 months vs. say 6 years. You can have a contest with another investor and your goals will be achieved in 9 months and he will have to wait 6 years—to achieve the SAME financial goals. Let that sink in for a second. You have your chips in 9 months. He has his in 6 years. Hmmm…

Put it another way. Using 'traditional' models of investing it will take you 5 times as long to achieve this level of wealth following traditional models or by following what I will be laying out here for you, you will be able to achieve your wealth 5 times faster!

Using my systems, what used to take 5–6 years now takes 9 months! <u>Read that again!</u>

What would you rather have?? Your chips in 9 months or in 6 years? Double your financial chips in 2 years or 12 years???

THIS IS THE MAIN REASON PEOPLE HIRE ME, AND PARTNER WITH ME FINANCIALLY. TO EITHER SPEED THE WEALTH BUILDING CYCLE UP FOR THEM, OR TO MAKE UP FOR LOST TIME SPENT ON THE TRADITIONAL MODELS OF THE PAST. AGAIN—TIME IS THE ENEMY.

PUTTING IT ANOTHER WAY… TO GET THEM THE RESULTS THEY WANT NOW VS. WAITING AND WAITING AND WAITING AND THEN *MAYBE* GETTING IT.

Look, I am not knocking down long term time perspective. I am not knocking down long term investing either. Heck, I have a portion of my Net Worth in the longer term type of traditional investments too.

Also, I am not advocating or really 'pitching' a get rich quick fix or band aid. These are all unrealistic and are used by snake oil salesmen. I am not advocating 'cheating' on your taxes, bilking your neighbor or finding the next Ponzi scheme or cheating the government, etc. I am not talking about anything illegal here either. I am talking about being smart and working smart. Being willing to do what most others will not or what most others will see as unconventional.

Like a mentor of mine says, 'Conventional behaviors produce conventional results. Unconventional behaviors produce outstanding results.'

What would you rather have? Yeah, me too. The outstanding results.

Oh, One More Problem We Have. (Sorry, I got to tell you about this stuff now!)

Then there comes the amount of time it takes to figure all this out yourself. I won't spend a lot of ink on this, but let's say it has taken me about 20 years to figure out how to get my wealth to grow at rocket speeds so, if you have a spare 20 years on you that you want to spend on this, feel free to expend the necessary energy.

Oh yeah, I almost forgot. The time expended when you make mistakes too. That's a biggie. Remember, to get good at anything you need to make a lot of mistakes first. Remember when you first learned how to ride a bike? Well, this book is like figuring out how to ride a bike the FIRST time you get on the darn thing and never having to fall off. Once again that darn TIME thing!

So, with all these said, and this chapter being on the subject of time, you will find this book very time friendly. The chapters are small, well marked, and easy to get through. The information is presented in plain English so even a third grader can understand what to do and how to do it. But most of all, it is presented so you can get results pretty quickly after reading this information. You can start applying this right away. Though not hundreds of pages this book is great stuff for those that are serious about fast wealth accumulation and seeing unconventional methods as a source of that achievement. This application can be used by anyone wishing to shrink time in order to achieve their financial goals through unconventional, yet legal and predictable means.

When it comes to this book, I have even done you a favor. I have blocked it off into three sections. **Section I deals with the Type of Investment That Will Accumulate Your Wealth Fast and take you to your wealth goal faster. Section II tells you what to do once you** have found that investment and the simple steps needed to get that investment running at full throttle and throwing off massive profits. Then there is Section III—what you need to do when it comes to selling the investment in order to guarantee huge cash windfalls and in some cases even tax deferred. So, no matter where you are in your investment cycle you will be able to use this book and its various sections over and over again.

Lastly, I even have a section in the back of the book to contact me for more resources in the event after reading this book you want to, well, deposit even more time in your time bank account and save even more time but get the results that you deserve....within months!

So, lets not waste any more time. On to the next chapter...

Right now before you forget, go to your computer and bookmark this website.

www.9monthinvestment.com

Chapter 2

The Biggest Tool In The Investment Toolbox

When it comes to a toolbox, you get a picture in your mind of just that, a tool box full of tools. Now, depending on your picture, this may be an organized tool box full of tools, or one that just has the tools thrown in there. Nevertheless, in your mind you probably see small tools like drill bits, screw drivers, wrenches, etc. and then you probably see some larger tools and some important tools like a hammer.

Then comes the tools you just have to have. There are many tools in the tool box that may get used every once in a while or maybe not even once a year. There are also tools that get used all of the time and are pretty important. In my toolbox, a tool that gets used rarely would be my plumbers wrench for pipes but the tool in the toolbox that would get used most would be the hammer.

When it comes to your wealth, I want you to think of the analogy of a toolbox. With your wealth you use lots of 'tools' with everything from checking and savings accounts, CD's, Mutual Funds, Money Markets, Savings Bonds, Etc - you get the picture. You have a lot of wealth building TOOLS in your wealth building tool box don't you? But again some tools are more important than others. For example a checking account is not going to be an investment that will increase your net worth substantially is it? No. It is a tool that you probably will use a lot but will not have THAT much of an effect on your net worth. But, there ARE tools in the tool box that will.

What I am going to talk about in this chapter is <u>THAT TOOL</u>! <u>THE tool</u> that you absolutely have to have in your toolbox in order to increase your wealth and net worth in the short 9 month time frame that I am talking about. Before I reveal this tool to you I need you to make me a promise. No prejudging. Hear me out. Why? Because on the surface you may think that this tool is not any big surprise, not any big revelation and I admit you will be right—it is not a secret of the ages that is just coming out. <u>BUT</u>, it's the way we will use this tool to get us the wealth that we are looking for in the short time frames.

The other way to think of this is that most wealth has been grown from non-traditional sources. In other words people are not getting or growing their wealth by using savings accounts, bank CD's or money market funds paying 1.2% interest.

So what is it? What is the tool that I have used and that my investment partners, friends and clients' use?

Apartment Buildings Requiring No Management By You! Well located, well maintained apartment buildings that increase in value and throw off cash flow in huge amounts AND they require no hands-on management by you!

Now, before we go any further, we need to cover a couple of important things here:

1. This is not a no money or low money down book or course. Far from it.
2. You will not have to know a lick about property management.
3. You will not have to know a lick about landlord 'stuff.'
4. You will not have to deal with any tenants…ever.
5. You will not have to spend time 'learning' how to be a landlord.
6. This is not complicated.

And remember, we are going to be investing in, holding, and selling these buildings in a short time frame—nine to eighteen months to be exact. So, again, this is not a buy the property and hold it and manage it for 30 years course. No Sireee!

Basically, you will be able to treat this with the same amount of time, stress, and energy as most any other 'conventional' investments, okay? My system stresses you **NOT** having to know or spend time on this stuff or learn how to become a landlord and fix toilets. No way. I spend zero time on this landlord stuff and you will spend the same amount of time on it - zero.

Do I have your attention? Good, because my system is going to take a simple apartment building investment and make it into a huge windfall for you, AND you are going to be able to do this over and over and over again.

Read the last paragraph again if you are not excited yet.

Okay, so I can hear the conversation at the back of your mind right now. "Okay Darin, so I can jump my wealth in huge amounts in short periods of time using apartment buildings AND I don't have to be a landlord to do it. Okay, sounds good so far, but Apartment Buildings? C'mon Darin I have seen enough of late night real estate snake oil salesmen to last a lifetime!"

Hold On—You will be glad you did—I promise. Give me just a minute here.

So, why apartment buildings?

Because apartment properties are one of the few investments that work overtime for you! 24/7 these properties are working for you and as you will see it is really four investments wrapped into one!

First, let's talk about investments working overtime for you. When you invest in a stock you are really hoping for ONE thing to happen—that it goes up in value right? It is strictly a capital gain type of investment isn't it? You buy the stock for $10.00 a share and hope it gets to $20.00 a share as soon as possible. You buy for $10.00, sell for $20.00 and pocket your profit. One kind of investment.

But not apartments. What if I told you that apartments are actually four investments working for you at the same time. That is right. Four!

When you buy an apartment property you will receive cash flow monthly from that apartment property. Once the rent comes in and the expenses are paid, the remaining cash flow goes into your pocket. At the same time you are getting this cash flow and pocketing it you are more than likely making a loan payment to a lender that loaned you the money to buy the building each month. What happens every month you make that loan payment? That loan balance goes down doesn't it? That is correct it goes down—every month. Who is making these loan payments? If you said that YOU were you are wrong my friend. The person that is REALLY making your loan payment for you is the tenant(s) isn't it? They are really the ones making the payment for you.

Then at the same time you are getting cash flow and your loan balance is being paid down what is that property doing every month? It is appreciating isn't it! Well located, well maintained apartment properties appreciate. So now you are not only having your loan balance go down each and every month with the tenants 'KIND' enough to pay those loan payments for you in the form of rent but you also have a property that is going UP in value at the same time! This of course creates equity and large amounts of it by the way. Equity is the key to our large net worth which I will get to in much more detail later. So our 'bank account' in this property gets larger and larger every single month!

Then, lastly, there is income tax savings. Yes income tax savings! When you own an apartment property Uncle Sam allows you to write off your expenses (there are ceilings that I will get to later). Uncle Sam allows you to write off daily wear and tear to the property as well as interest in your loan that the tenants pay for you as well as your other expense like property taxes, insurance, maintenance, etc.

Why is this good?

Because you can have say a $10,000 a year cash flow coming from the property into your pocket BUT when you file your tax return and write off these expenses you can legally show you made little profit or in some cases zero profit from the property. This is legal! Nothing like having an income of $10,000 and not be taxed on it.

Lastly, Uncle Sam also allows us to sell our property and defer paying any taxes on the sale for as long as we want! Apartments are one of the few investments that when sold allow you to roll over ALL of your capital gains taxes from the sale of the property into your next investment and legally defer all of those taxes! How would you like to sell your 5,000 shares of ABC company and defer those taxes? You would like it I am sure, but guess what? You can't.

Frankly, what kind of investment is there that can do so many things for you? It is really like a bunch of little investments all wrapped up into one isn't it? This is the base of our power to increase our net worth fast. Have as many of these 'investments in an investment' working for us at once. When you have these many investments wrapped up into one investment it means faster than average wealth building.

This is the base of my system. Using this leverage over and over again. Now, before you run off half cocked and invest in the first apartment property you find there are MANY other items you need to know and be aware of for my system to work, so hold on and keep reading.

For now, be content that Step 1 is investing in a well located, well maintained apartment property. We have much more to cover but this is the start.

Before we end this chapter, I want you to know at the end of each chapter I will be providing a step-by-step guide for you to refer to. This online guide will take you step-by-step through the process of owning a fantastic property that will increase in value and cash flow fast. You must follow this system and formula for this to work; otherwise you will just be another owner of another apartment property having average results. Also, I will have other online resources you can refer to as well.

Remember, we don't want average, we want above average!!

With that said:

Step 1–Your 9 Month Investment Will Be In A Well Located, Well Maintained Apartment Property. You can also download your own apartment property planning journal and business plan at www.9monthinvestment.com.

CHAPTER 3

THE INEXPERIENCED APPROACH TO WHAT KIND OF APARTMENTS TO INVEST IN AND WHAT TO AVOID. IT'S ACTUALLY REALLY SIMPLE.

The good news is that the process of knowing what kind of apartments to invest in and which to avoid, in order to reach those financial goals in no time is pretty simple.

What a lot of people or supposed 'experts' would do in describing what kinds of apartment properties you should be buying and should be avoiding is to go into 5 chapters of minutiae that for our purposes is not necessary. You would get the tips and strategies for inspections, negotiations on this stuff, who your power team should be, how to deal with owners, appraisers, real estate brokers, etc. etc.

Remember, we are not interested in learning how to be experts at the mechanics of this—we just want the results of an expert and we want to know what we need to do and not do. Period. If you want more information than that I would recommend that you become a professional real estate investor. I mean it is the results you are after isn't it?

But again, this book is about getting the results of an expert without committing the time to become one right!

With that said and with our goal being to be in an apartment property that will produce the large leaps in our net worth in 3-9 months here are some very important tips for you:

What Kind of Apartment Properties To Avoid:

When you start your search you need to avoid the following apartment properties:

1. Government subsidized housing or tax credit housing.
2. City subsidized housing.
3. Any housing with an FHA loan.
4. Any FMHA housing.
5. Converted Housing (was once a house now a 10 unit sleeping room house)
6. Converted Housing Commercial (was once a warehouse now condos)
7. Single Family Homes
8. Low Income Housing in Low Income Neighborhoods or C class property.
9. New Construction.

I am not going to take the time and go over each one of these in great detail and give you the reasons to avoid each one. It is enough to know from my experience that this is the list you should commit to but I will hit on each briefly just so you do have an idea as to where I am coming from.

In a nutshell the main reason you want to avoid the majority of these is because of government regulation. Even though the government does not own the property they sure think they do. So when the government owns the property and makes the decisions (not you) run away from those. Most of those in the top 4 are some kinds of government housing that carry too much risk.

Number 5 and 6 are just headaches. Conversions can look good on paper but their profits after paying higher than average utility and maintenance expenses are ones you should avoid. Also, the resale is terrible.

Number 7 may be a small surprise. Single family homes are easy to manage but their cash flow it typically terrible and unless you are in the business of flipping homes, you will not be able to get the large increases in value in a short period of time that we can get from apartment buildings unless you buy at a huge, huge discount.

With number 8, it's about resale again. Hard to sell a property in a neighborhood that is mainly low income. I wish it was not that way but it is. Think about it—want a property in a great location with job holding tenants or want something that has a police substation on most corners?? Hard to sell.

You may be surprised by #9. Don' t be. When a developer builds an apartment property they usually have to come out of the ground with top of the market rents in order for the property to work or again, you have to deal with governmental rent subsidy. You cannot do much in the way of adding value to a property when the rents are already about as high as they can go. Not much in the way of 'upside' here. So, avoid these too.

Now that we have that out of the way let's talk about what kind of apartment property you should invest in:

1. Properties built as apartment properties.
2. Apartments located in economically strong areas.
3. Apartments with economically strong tenants.
4. Properties of 12 units or more.
5. Class 'B' or better properties 7–25 years of age.

My bread and butter are properties that are 7–25 years of age. These are usually where you will find the better deals since this is the broadest category of the 'financially neglected' property we want to find or have our expert (as we will talk about in a later chapter) find for us.

The good news for you is, you now have a requirement list to not only go by when you are reviewing apartment projects that we find on our own or our expert gets in front of us, (again more on that later) but this approach also saves you a lot of time! Knowing what your criteria IS will automatically get you the project that will work for you FASTER. Why? You are using a focused approach and avoiding wasting time on the properties that will not work.

You see, when I first got in the business I spent a lot of time looking at property that in the end did not come close to my criteria. The phone calls, inspections, time in the car and with brokers or owners that I have wasted on properties that did not even come close to working is huge—not just wasted hours but when added up would be days! I get sick when I think about it.

But not you. You are focused right now. You now know what kind of apartment property you want to own and the kind to avoid.

5 Key Strategies For Your 9 Month Profit In Apartment Ownership

I have gone over what you should be looking for and what you should be avoiding. I know it sounds simple and I know that I have shared with you may not be all that earth shattering but I guarantee you I have made you at least $100,000 in profits by going over this with you. Just knowing this simple 'what to buy and what to avoid' list will put a minimum of 6 figures in your pocket.

Now that we have that firmly in mind, let's expand to what I call my Power Strategies. These will expand on what I just went over but will be very valuable to you as you start looking at apartment properties for sale...

Apartment Investor Power Strategies:

1. **Buy Only Apartments Built As Apartment Properties:** Only invest in projects built as apartment properties. Do NOT invest in weird conversions okay? If they were not out of the ground as an apartment property, my friend, run away from it. Keep in mind that these properties will look good on paper but they will be a nightmare to own and to sell. No way!

2. **Buy An Apartment Property ONLY In An Strong Economic City and Area.** This is an easy one. Don't be like my friend who bought a 16-unit in a city with a population of about 700 people. The building he bought was fully occupied when he bought it but only to find out 8 months later he was 50% vacant. What happened? His manager told him they stopped

building the ethanol plant so all the workers left. By the way that was 2 years ago!!! He is still 50% occupied and looking for tenants in this small town! Economy has got to be good where your apartment property is or you run fast - Okay?

3. **Buy An Apartment With Economically Strong Tenants.** You want tenants that are working, okay? A test for you is to do your inspection in the daytime around 10 am. If you are just 'driving the property' notice how many cars are there and what they look like. If the parking lot is full and there are a lot of people 'hanging out' on the site at 10 am that is a bad sign. If you plan on looking at the interior of the property if the tenant is either still in bed or watching TV, again at 10 AM, that is not necessarily a bad thing BUT if most of the tenants are doing this it is a sign you have a problem and run away from that too. If they are watching Jerry Springer instead of working no dice, okay?

4. **Buy Apartments of 12 units or more**. Bottom line here is the larger the property, the larger the jump in property value. Small property small jumps, big properly big jumps. Keep it to a minimum of 12 so you can have large enough jumps in value that will make this worthwhile.

5. **Class B Properties or Better**. Look, you want nice properties. Avoid the junk, okay! Properties are rated from A, B and C. Of course A is the best property in the best location and in the best condition. B property is average properties in average locations and condition. C Properties are crappy properties in crappy areas of the city. You want a B property or better!

This is a pretty uncomplicated way to look at apartments isn't it? Well, remember, that is our point, to make sure you understand that you can really grow your wealth in a huge way in the short term buy NOT having this be complicated. In this chapter if you understand what to find and what to avoid you are already 70% of the way there!

Step 2–Make sure you only purchase or invest in apartments that meet our criteria that we have stated here in this book. Do not alter course on this. You will be tempted to do so but in the long run this is your best course of action to large and faster profits. You can download the list of what kind of apartments to purchase and what kind to avoid by going to www.9monthinvestment.com.

CHAPTER 4

FINDING LEVERAGE AND PROFITING HANDSOMELY. HAVING SOMEONE ELSE DO THE HEAVY LIFTING FOR YOU.

Delegating has never been this profitable!!

As we talked about previously, you do not have the time, effort or energy to become a real estate expert but you can profit like one nonetheless. This book is about getting the results of an expert without having to spend hours, months or even in some cases years on this. Again, we don't want to take the time to be the Expert but we want the results of an expert.

Your job now is to find the expert in your market on apartment properties. You want to find the 'Darin Garman' of your market if you will. More than likely, this will be a commercial real estate broker. Again, we are not just looking for any broker or agent that has a real estate license. No way! We want THE EXPERT in the apartment market. Simply put, we want to find them and have them work for us...Bringing us deal after deal that meets our previously discussed criteria. We want our experts to spend their time on this and do the heavy lifting for us.

How? How do we find the apartment market expert and MAKE SURE that we have the right person working for us and bringing us the most profitable deals in the shortest period of time??

How do we find this guy to give our criteria to and do the heavy lifting for us in the first place AND feel confident that this IS the guy that we can trust?

It is not as difficult as you may think. Really, if you can spend an hour on the phone I guarantee you will be able to find the expert you want—yes, with just one hour on the phone. How??? It's very easy. Remember, I know because I am one.

How To Find The Expert That Will Make You Millions.

What you do is obtain a list of the top three to five banks in the market you plan on investing. Again, this can be in your market or any of the other market(s) you want to be located in. This would be the top three to five banks you feel are the largest banks in the city and/or the biggest players in the commercial real estate financing market.

For example, lets just say you live in Wichita Kansas and in Wichita the lenders are Wells Fargo, US Bank and Bank of the West.

You call these lenders cold and tell the receptionist that you want to speak with a commercial lending officer about financing a large number of apartments. He or she will put you through to someone.

Once you get through and get the person on the phone here is how your conversation should go:

Bank Officer: Hello this is Mark Fields

You: Hi Mark, Darin Garman here with Garman properties. The reason I am calling you is that we are looking at purchasing 100–200 units in the (their city) market in the next 90 days or so and wanted to see if we should be talking with you guys about financing.

Bank Officer: Sure, yes, we like apartments, etc., etc. They will be all smiles on the phone at this juncture.

You: Can you give me an idea, in general, what type of rate, terms, loan to values, etc. I would typically see from you guys for apartments locally?

Bank Officer: Will go over their criteria, lending philosophy, etc, etc. Listen politely and if you want jot down what they are saying. It's not mandatory that you do.

You: Great that helps a lot. Say, who do you guys use for appraisals of your apartment properties you finance—you know—that knows the market and has experience? Is there an individual or company I should know about?

Bank Officer: Will tell you your answer. Write this down.

You: After you take down the information you ask one more question, "Who is the 'go to' real estate broker for apartments in the city? In your opinion, who is the person that can assist us in finding a good property?"

Bank Officer: Will probably give you two or three contacts. WRITE THESE DOWN!

You: Hey, last question for you I promise. Who do you recommend as a good real estate attorney and property management company?

Bank Officer: They will answer. Write these down.

You: Hey, Thanks for the information I appreciate it and I will be in touch.

Now, what you have done in a brief phone call is get an idea of the people that will probably know more about the apartment market you want to be in, an appraiser(s) and or a Broker(s). Now, the lender may want to get your contact info, etc. and go ahead and oblige them - you MAY need them later.

Again, make sure you do this at least three times and talk to at least three commercial lenders and run through the same questions, okay??

Once you are done with this little phone exercise you should have 3 to 6 appraisers and 3 to 6 brokers recommended by the lenders.

Now, we are NOT done yet!!

We have just a few more calls to make.

Your next series of calls will now be to the appraiser(s) that your bank friends have recommended. Again, once you talk to two or three lenders you should have about 3 to 6 names of appraisers that come up more often than not.

Anyway, you call these appraisers that were recommended by your friendly bankers.

Once you get a hold of them on the phone, you tell them that *you talked to a couple of lenders in the city and they recommended that you talk to them about the apartment market*. If you get just a company name tell the receptionist this verbatim and then ask him or her who you should talk to in the office. If you got the name of the appraiser then of course ask for him or her.

Again, just like the bankers you let them know that you plan on purchasing a large amount of apartments in the next 6 to 12 months and you would like to ask them a few quick questions about the market.

They will of course oblige you since you said they were recommended by a couple of top lenders.

However, here is what I want your first question to be after the warm up:

You: Hey, before I forget, whom do you recommend for a good real estate broker that knows a lot about the local apartment market here?

Now, bankers will have a good idea as to this question and that is why you asked them, however, if these guys are really competent real estate appraisers they will really know who you need to be talking to because many times they will get the information they use for the appraisals from the real estate brokers that sold the apartment property in the first place.

You: After you take down the information on the commercial real estate broker:

Okay, great. What can you tell me about the average *capitalization rates right now for B type properties or better?

*(capitalization rates are the measuring stick of apartment value. The capitalization rate or 'cap' rate is the NET income of the property divided by its value OR what your return would be on a property if

you paid ALL CASH for it. For example: the selling price of a property is $500,000. The Net Income was $50,000. Your cap rate is 10% - $50,000 Net Income divided by the $500,000 sales price = 10%.)

They will tell you and give you a number. Write this number down.

Then ask them: If we wanted to purchase a larger project but not more than 200 units about how long do you think the process would take in this market?

They will answer that question as well. (By the way, feel free to adjust the unit number up or down based on the size of your market—New York I would go up but Belle Plaine, Iowa I would go down!)

You: Last question I promise. Who are the sharpest real estate attorneys and property management companies in town?

The appraiser will tell you and once they do, thank them for their time. Feel free to tell them you hope to work with them in the future and that they have been helpful.

Remember, you ask these same questions for every appraiser that you talk to, okay?

Now that you have had these conversations with these appraisers and lenders now you have a nice amount of important information that will come in very handy.

But wait, we're not done yet.

Put your notes together. So far you have only about two hours invested in this and you have gotten a lot accomplished! You now have recommendations of commercial brokers from not only lenders but from appraisers. You will of course have 2 to 3 of them that names come up over and over again and are used by both the appraisers and lenders. You now have your short list of commercial broker go to guys in the market place don't you? You bet!

And, you have some information on capitalization rates and the time it is probably going to take to find a project that makes sense to you. So far so good.

Okay, what now?

You go ahead now and call those 2 to 3 commercial brokers whose name kept coming up when you were talking to the lenders and the appraisers and here is what you say:

You: You first let them know that they were recommended to you by a couple of bankers and appraisers. Then you tell them that you are interested in purchasing up to 200 units in the next year and wondering if they could help you.

Of course they will say sure.

Then you simply ask them four questions.

1. The question again, from before, about what are cap rates doing now on class B property and better and what can you expect to pay.

And

2. How long do they think it will take you to find a property.

3. Who do they recommend for a real estate attorney, property management company and accounting firm?

Then you ask these brokers the all important question. Here it is:

4. In your opinion, who is the 'mover and shaker' in the market here in terms of apartment property ownership. Who is the guy with the most experience as a successful apartment owner?

Trust me, they will know. If they give you some large company make sure you ask them for someone local. They will give you at least one name.

These will be people that you will want to be rubbing elbows with since they actually OWN the real estate.

You have now narrowed the following very important items down and all it took you was 1–2 hours on the phone.

1. **Go To Lenders**
2. **Go To Appraisers**
3. **Go To Real Estate Brokers**
4. **Local Market Gurus**

This is fantastic!

Remember, we are doing this because we want to build our wealth faster. Also, we do not want to spend the time, effort, money, or energy in becoming the experts ourselves - not enough time to do that right? But, look what we have accomplished so far. We now have the market experts assembled and ready to help us; ready to give us some serious leverage.

In about 1 to 2 hours of time on the phone we now know, with some good recommendations, who the 'go to guys' are in the market that can make you wealthy using this vehicle called apartments. Done any other way it would have taken you forever and you would have probably got hooked up with the wrong folks. So, even though you are not in a project yet as an owner go ahead and pat yourself on the back! You have just saved yourself months of time and thousands of dollars in the process!

Step 3–Remember, once you know what kind of apartments to find and what kind to avoid, now you need as many of the apartments that work to cross your desk at once as possible. Immediately hire the most competent real estate broker in the market to assist you in finding these properties. Let the real estate broker do the heavy lifting while you have a life.

Base your decision on who should work for you by number of years of experience, what their annual sales volume is, and how you feel interacting with these guys on the phone. The more experience and the more they sell, the more products they can get in front of you and most of it before it even hits the market. I have a broker questionnaire that you can download and use at www.9monthinvestment.com.

CHAPTER 5

THE SECRET PROFIT FORMULA THAT WILL PUT HUNDREDS OF THOUSANDS OF DOLLARS IN YOUR POCKET.

The good news is that after Chapter 4 you should have the market expert in your back pocket that will be bringing deals to you for your review while you are doing other things. You have a commercial broker team (and more than one is okay) that really knows the market and can cut through the proverbial crap and get some real gems for you - faster and with less hassle. You have identified the 'Go To' lenders, banks, appraisers and brokers and it took you a whopping 1.5 hours to do it! Good work! It takes most people 6 months or more to be in this position and many STILL do not know what to do. Gotta like that leverage!

But there is just one detail that you have to work out yet—before you get started.

What criteria do you (and your broker) need to follow to guarantee that only the right projects get put in front of you? Or, put another way now that you know that smart apartment investing is the faster way to wealth in the next 9 months what kind of apartment properties should you work to avoid what kind of properties do you look for to profit from?

You see you DO already have criteria mainly about what your property should be constructed as and where it should be located. So far, we really have not talked about any financial numbers of the properties that need to be considered.

So, once you and your broker have found the apartment property that passes our litmus test in Chapter 3 there is one more part of the test. I call this, not surprisingly, **The Investment Formula**.

Here is your Investment Formula Criteria:

The property needs to be:

1. Not on the 'What to Avoid' list From Chapter Three.
2. On Your 'Where to Invest' list From Chapter Three.
3. Total Rents of ALL THE UNITS COMBINED Are Currently 9% or more under market rent.
4. Total Current COMBINED Expenses (not including loan payments, interest or depreciation) Are 9% or more HIGHER than they really need to be.

It's pretty simple, really as I told you earlier this would be. All you need to do is work on NOT buying a property on the what to avoid list and work on buying a property on the where you should own list that has rents that are at least 9% under market and expenses that can be cut realistically in 9 months or less by 9%.

As you can see the magic number here is 9%. Anytime you can get movement of 9% or more in an apartment property in terms of income growth and expense reduction you have a winner. Even though 9% does not seem like that much when you do these two items at the same time (income and expenses) it spells huge profits for you.

Let me give you and example:

Forest Arms Apartments

(Assume it meets our 'Avoid' and 'Where and What to Buy' List Criteria)

Gross Annual Income: $80,000
Annual Expenses: $40,000
Net Income: $40,000

CURRENT Value at a 10% Capitalization Rate: $400,000

Now, to fast forward a bit to show you how powerful this is, lets say we have identified this property as one that is at least 9% under market rents (the rents can easily go up 9%) and 9% too much in expenses (you can realistically cut the expenses of 9%).

Assume now for simplicity sake you buy this property and in 12 months time you raise the rents 9% to market levels and lower your expenses by 9% at the same time. Here is what your income stream would look like:

After 9% Transformation

Gross Income: $87,200
Expenses: $36,400
Net Income: $50,800

REAL Value at a 10% Capitalization Rate: $508,000!

You just made $100,000+ in less than 12 months and all you did was raise rents and reduce expenses. Have I talked about fix up or rehab? Not once—again—we avoid those properties. Also, you probably had some cash flow coming from the units during this time period as well. Not bad huh?

You think this is good…just think if you do this with a $4,000,000 property you would have over $1,000,000 in profit—again—for just increasing income and reducing expenses by a measly 9%!!!

This is why apartments are the way to go. You can make millions in profits and not have to go to college for 4–12 years in order to earn this kind of money. You can start earning this today—in your own back yard. All you need to do is know your numbers. ***This IS Exciting!!***

So here is how you use this formula when you look at apartment projects once you have them in front of you. Remember if your broker is doing a good job these should ALREADY meet your rule of 9% criteria.

Your Punch List

1. If submitted by a broker does the apartment property meet the rule of 9%?

2. If you are not sure do your own analysis to see if it does indeed meet the rule of 9%.

3. Figure out how much the property is worth NOW with the current income stream using the current prevailing market capitalization (cap) rate—remember we find this out by talking to our 'go to' appraisers and brokers.

4. Figure out how much the property would be worth with the NEW income stream (9% rules on income and expenses) using current market cap rate.

5. Figure out your gross profit.

6. Figure out any costs if you decide to sell it like brokerage fees, costs of sale, etc.

7. Does the property need any work completed in order for the sale to happen faster? If so estimate what those costs will be.*

8. Take the answer to 5 and subtract the answer to 6 and then 7 to get your net profit.

*Remember, we are not into doing rehab jobs since we want nice average to above average properties in the same kind of locations. There may be occasions where you will do some painting, landscaping, etc. but avoid rehab jobs.

Again you want to remember to not become discouraged because many projects will NOT meet your criteria so you need to keep moving on until you find a project that does!

Your expert will be bringing you about 2 or 3 projects a month that will come close and even though that does not sound like very many, it is pretty good because you do not need very many properties in order to fold time—remember—that is our ultimate goal! It only takes one of these babies to really pay off!

Dealing with Your Broker and Your Formula...Getting Fast Action and Fast Results

Since you will be spending quite a bit of time talking to commercial real estate brokers let's take this time to talk about how to deal with brokers. First, do not look at brokers as a pain or an impediment to a deal. Good brokers know the market, properties and owners well and can give you very good insight into the apartment market not only when you look but during negotiations as well.

Many people think that brokers are always in the way, and a pain as well. Again, do not take this approach. If you use and leverage them—especially since you should have the top one(s) ready to work for you—it will save you an unbelievable amount of time, money and frustration. Remember, it's all about leverage!

But how do we get these brokers to bring us projects, consistently, after we identify who they are? Here are your steps:

1. Meet with all of them and tell them you are looking at purchasing an apartment project—up to 200 units—in the next 90–120 days. Go over your criteria with them on what you are looking for.

2. Ask them about how they plan on going about working with you and helping you locate these projects. You want to be the one that gets first shot at these projects so how do they put you in that position? You want to be in the position to see what no one else can see.

3. If the broker requires you to sign an exclusive representation agreement I recommend doing so as long as it gives you a way out in the event the broker does not live up to the expectations you have both discussed. Make sure it is no longer than 6 months in length.

What Your Broker Should Look Like.

I know sounds funny doesn't it? What your broker should look like? Well, I am not talking looks here, I am talking experience. Your brokers should have:

A) Sold at least $20,000,000 in just apartments over the years.
B) Own or has owned apartments themselves.
C) Has a 'Go to Guy' reputation in the city. (Applies to female brokers as well)

This is ideal. When you have someone that is working for you (at no cost by the way, since typically the seller pays the brokers fee) that has great experience in the market you are in AND also owns apartments themselves (or has owned them) you are dealing with someone that can spot a great deal for you. This is IDEAL!

What to Avoid In a Broker

Make sure that you avoid working with a broker with little or no experience. If you have a friend or a friend of a friend that is a residential agent do yourself a favor and do NOT work with them. I have seen so many investors make huge investment mistakes by getting hooked up with the wrong broker. Make sure that this is not you. Use the A, B and C litmus test above—please!

Also your broker does NOT need to be with or affiliated with a big national real estate company either. This is another mistake. Do not think that just because they are affiliated with a big national brokerage company that they are good. Many are not. Again, make sure they pass the ABC test above before you chat with them.

The Other Members of Your Team

Many commercial real estate gurus talk about a power team. Really, no difference here. You will want to have these folks on your team as well.

1. Good CPA
2. Good Attorney
3. Good Property Management Company.
4. Good Broker.

Again, this is about leverage! We want all of these people to do the heavy lifting for us! Now, I have already talked about how important a good broker is to you and you finding deals. I won't spend much time on CPA's and attorneys. Just make sure that the CPA and attorney that you use are again, experienced in real estate—specifically commercial real estate. It's a plus if they own property as well, or have owned property. The attorney that I use owns commercial real estate himself and the CPA that I use has a ton of experience with commercial real estate matters. A good source of a referral for who you should talk to would be your commercial broker(s). The other place are other owners that you will be talking to from time to time as well—who do THEY use??

I will deal with property management later since it is very important to how fast your property will increase in value. Keep in mind that I don't want you to be a property management expert and deal with tenants at all - I just want you to choose a very good expert to do the heavy lifting for you. Management is key to large property value increases so I will be spending an entire chapter just on that but for now there is NO excuse for you to not have the areas top apartment broker bringing you deal after deal.

Step 4—Qualify the property using the Secret Formula "Rule of 9%". Once that is done, make sure that you use leverage in terms of real estate brokers and the other members of your real estate investment team. At www.9monthinvestment.com there are broker and vendor checklists to use to shortcut the process as to whom you should work with as well as "Rule of 9%" Checklists to use!

CHAPTER 6

THE IMPORTANCE OF PROPER INSPECTIONS.

Remember, your offer is always contingent upon the inspection and acceptance of all units, grounds, and property, both structurally and environmentally. Now that you have negotiated the price and terms of the deal, it's time to look at the property. Also remember this important question as you start inspecting the units:

What do the units look like and can we get the units rented for the market rent AS IS? If not—what do we need to do to the units and the property to get that? This needs to be your attitude going into the inspection part of any apartment property. It does not matter if YOU would live there.

Remember, our goal here is to NOT spend a lot of money in fix up work on the property. We are not in the business of rehab. So, when you look at the property and the units you want to make note of the things you will need to do to the property to make it more valuable or saleable in the next 9 months. We are not looking at doing many (if any) upgrades to the property because we know we can rent the units for more money than they are producing now <u>without</u> doing anything to the units in the first place.

Example. We just got done looking at a 12 unit property. Units were renting for $520 per month. Based on the CURRENT CONDITION OF THOSE UNITS we know we can rent these units for $575 in the next 12 months. Now, some units may need the carpets cleaned, linoleum repaired, some minor items fixed, replaced or a paint job in the unit but that is about it. Just some sprucing up.

Another example A while ago we looked at a 7 unit property and each of the units were renting for $195.00 as is. We know we could get $335 per unit as is.

Again, this is based on the current condition of those units.

To be clear…

We want a property where the current tenant is paying a discount in rent vs. what we know the unit could rent for. We do not want a property that we have to refurbish and spend tens of thousands of dollars in order to make money.

So the majority of your inspection time will be spent on the following:

1. How much is the current tenant paying for the apartment in rent?
2. How much can the rent be for the apartment in "as is" condition?
3. How quickly can we get to market rent?
4. How much work (if any) is needed to get the unit to the state of being able to easily get market rent?

Now, you will have some units that may need a little bit of work. Maybe some carpet replaced here, a new paint job there, new stove here, new refrigerator there. Also, you may have a property where the common areas just need a little sprucing up. Maybe the hallways need a new coat of paint? Maybe the landscaping around the building needs to be touched up? You get the picture. We are interested in sprucing up the cosmetics of the property AT THE MOST!

Again, we are not only inspecting the condition of the property but we are also inspecting the units too see if we can get more rent for those units than the current owner is getting and what, if anything, do we need to do in order to get top of the market rents.

Step 5—Now is the time to see if your suspicions are correct and see if this apartment property is a real winner. Are you going to be able to raise the rents of the apartments in their existing condition and if so how much? Will some work be required? Is the current owner renting at a discount? For a checklist to use while you are going on your property inspections you can down load this at www.9monthinvestment.com.

Chapter 7

How To Find Owners That Want To Work With You—FAST!

First remember, you have your broker(s) working for you bringing you deals. Depending on how serious you are about getting rich from this or just having this be a nice additional source of income for you from time to time; you may just stop here and have your broker do all of the work for you and just have them check in with you or keep you on their HOT LIST. This is fine as long as you understand that you will not get as many deals crossing your desk by just doing it this way. In any case—it's up to you. You can have them do the heavy lifting for you and that is it.

Also, remember from our previous chapters, I said that some of the best owners to work with and get good discounts on apartments from, whether they know it or not, are out of state or out of town apartment owners.

What I want to focus on in this chapter is really how to get more results faster—really—how to get as many owners wanting to work with you as quickly as possible. What this will entail is more work on your part, but if it is speed that you desire it will be well worth the effort.

Of course I already mentioned one way to get as many apartment projects in front of you is to have a successful broker working for you. Another way to get the heavy lifting done for you is to team up with me and my Private Partners in our future apartment project purchases (more on this later). But if you really want to leverage this I have some ideas for you…that work!

The Power of Direct Mail!

The other way to get some responses is to directly mail the owners of apartment properties. On my website I have the exact letter you should be using to send to the owners of apartment properties in your city. I have used this letter successfully for years and it brings in results year after year. So, in broad terms, all you need to do is have your broker bring you deals, and mail this letter out to owners of apartment properties in your city.

Couple of quick notes on this however.

1. Make sure that you send out letters ONLY to property owners that own the kind of properties that pass our litmus test. No use in sending these letters to people that own the converted old shack built in 1844. Waste of time and money.

2. Make sure you send the letter to them every month.

3. On Letters Working. Keep in mind that you will not get a huge response when you mail these out. I know, I said the letters work and they do but remember this is more of a timing thing than anything else. One month the owner may have no interest in selling but 6 months from now his niece may need a heart transplant. That is why you must do this as I have outlined.

If you get 5 responses out of 100 every time you mail these letters you are doing fantastic. Heck, even 2 responses are good! Why? How can I say that only 2 responses out of 100 are good? Because of the pay off! Remember, you do NOT need a large number of people to respond in order to make money—you only need ONE DEAL to double or triple your net worth. Remember that. Many people start to get discouraged if after sending 100 letters out they do not get 30 to respond. DON'T WORRY ABOUT IT! We can get rich off of small numbers.

4. Where Do You Get The Owners Names And Addresses For Sending These Done For You Letters? The first place you go to is your title company in your city. They should have a list of apartment owners in your city that is readily available either

free or they may charge you a small fee—don't complain—pay it! It is well worth the money. If you check the title company and they do not have this information then you go the property tax assessor's office. The tax assessor should have a list of all apartment owners in your city as well and may even be able to break it down by number of units, location, value, etc. Usually they have a computer you can go to and look for the information yourself. Lastly, if you fail on both of these tries contact your city rental housing inspection office. Most cities have a housing inspection office and of course these folks have all the information on all of the apartments in the city since they do the housing inspections on them. These folks should have a list of owners and addresses. Of course you can also hire someone for $7.00 an hour to do this for you as well.

5. Be consistent and remember every deal will not work out. Expect the best out of every project, but do not get too down if it does not work out. Just because someone gets back to you and responds does not mean their property will meet your criteria in the end either. Don't let this get you down—remember—if it was all that easy you would not be reading this book—you would be doing it too right? You will have to wade through some garbage to get to the good stuff. The key is to keep wading.

6. The direct mail program is easy but you must be consistent. I have an entire sequence of easy to use three step letters that I send to apartment property owners in my area that convinces them, at least at some time, to get in touch with me. The key is to do this every two weeks (three times) and not just a shotgun approach and then do nothing. (if you want to get information on my total three step letter system to send then simply go to www.9monthinvestment.com) The Key? Getting and keeping in touch with these owners consistently and letting them know that you are interested in their property when the time is right for them to sell and are actually at a point to want to hear what you have to say, which brings me to one more important point.

7. These owners will be ready to sell and talk to you when THEY are ready not when YOU are ready. Look, if you are like me you are ready for ALL of the BUSINESS RIGHT NOW! We all are like that. Unfortunately, it does not work out like that. Always keep in mind that just because you are ready does not mean the owners should be or are ready. This is both good news and bad news for you. The bad news is that most people are NOT READY to sell at any given moment, so, you will not get huge responses to your mailings. Odds are the vast majority of apartment owners, whenever they get our materials or hear from you will NOT be ready to sell. BUT THE GOOD NEWS is that the ones that do respond will be at a point of being motivated and will be ready to sell and in some cases at a nice profit to you. This is who you want to deal with isn't it? Someone that IS ready!! Someone that IS motivated? You are able to cut better deals that way.

Now, don't get me wrong you will have people contact you more curious in what you are up to vs. selling their building(s) and these people will be a pain and may even discourage you. Again—DON'T get discouraged. If you follow my simple 1 letter a month for 12 months contact program—just via the mail—with the owners of properties in your area you will be real estate rich within 12 months. I guarantee it!!

Again—back to what I said before. You do not need a large response to make a lot of money with this. I love large numbers! Between having brokers working for you and you doing this yourself, you will have enough leads coming in to make life interesting for you with many potential ways to profit. Again, a reminder from 'Uncle Darin' - before you get too excited always remember your criteria! It is VERY easy to forget the reason you are doing this anyway—to make money on properties that meet our 9% criteria. Let me illustrate:

I just had a friend call me—his name is Rick. Rick owns a 4-unit building in my city and called to see if I would have an interest in buying it. The property is an old converted home needing a lot of repair. Based on what I thought, I could sell his building for Rick did not like my number. He thought he could get a higher sales price. Not that much of a surprise—most owners feel this way. Anyway, I told him that he needed to raise his rents and reduce his expenses before he could get more for the property. Here is what he said, "I really did not buy that building to make a lot of money—I have been happy with it basically just paying for itself year after year." Huh? Rick, you mean you did not go through the hassle of being an apartment owner to make money? I will talk more in the next chapter about this but make sure you ARE in it for the money—AT ALL TIMES! Far too many people make this mistake and get caught up in other emotional issues as it relates to tenants and it costs them a lot of money and time—let's make sure this is not you okay? Again, more on this in the next chapter…but keep in mind it needs to meet our criteria!

Before we leave this chapter you have been given the easy to follow process of getting apartment property owners and brokers to deliver properties to you consistently. Again, you can just sit back and have your broker specializing in apartments do this for you or you can double the amount of apartments coming to you by also doing a bit of work yourself. Once you have this process operating effectively, you will now start to see a nice stream of properties cross your desk.

Last note on this chapter. Remember you will need to do SOME work on this, however, what we are talking about here is very, very easy to do isn't it? Just find the owners, send them letters and see the results come in? I will talk more about that in the next chapter.

Now that you have this process going and working for you it is time to make sure you do not fall victim to one simple mistake that will wipe out all of your progress to this point and in the future. I will deal with that in the next chapter.

Step 6—Using my simple to follow strategies, you can have a stream of apartment projects coming to you for your review month after month. You can sit back and just have your qualified apartment specialist real estate broker doing this for you, or you can double the amount of apartment properties coming to you by implementing my simple three step letter campaign. Remember, just a few of these apartment properties will double or triple your net worth over the next 2 to 3 years. You can tap into these resources to help you right now by going to www.9monthinvestment.com.

CHAPTER 8

ARE YOU A SOCIAL WORKER OR AN INVESTOR?

Okay, it's time to take a quick timeout from the strategies and implementation parts of my system to make sure you stay on track and avoid a common and costly mistake. Let's call this a profitable detour.

Last chapter, I referred to much of your progress being stalled by committing this mistake and I also mentioned the brief story of Rick and how he told me that he was not in this for the money.

The main reason you picked up this book or purchased it online is more than likely because of its title. The 9 month investment is just that—making as much progress in growing your net worth in 9 months vs. 5 to 10 years. The information that you are reading will really help you to that end. Always keep this in mind. You are doing this for profit! FAST PROFITS!

Now, along the way if you help some people—all the better. But remember—helping people is NOT the reason you are doing this. You are doing this for profit—Not to be your own social organization. If you want to help people contribute to your favorite charity or volunteer, etc. DON'T USE THESE METHODS TO GET RICH FAST TO NOT GET RICH. Huh??

I have seen it time and time again. At the end of the last chapter I talked to you about a guy named Rick and how after over 10 years of owning and managing an apartment building himself—he really did not make any money doing it. As a matter of fact one of his tenants has NOT had their rent raised in over 10 years! Can you imagine paying the same rent for 10 years?? From a tenant standpoint that would of course be great, but from an owner's standpoint not so much. The other thing I found out from Rick was that the other tenants have only gotten a rent increase here and there over the last 10 years with no real strategy to it—he just did it when he thought it may be a good time to do it. As of the writing of this book, Rick's rents are still about $100+ under market for his units. That is a profit of $400 per month he is missing out on or $4,800 per year!

So here is the question. Why does Rick not raise those rents—especially after 10 years?? I mean if you were missing out on about $5,000 per year in profit and cash flow that you could easily have wouldn't you? Believe it or not many people would NOT and in this case Rick chose not to.

Why?

Because Rick is a HELPER not an INVESTOR! Rick was afraid to raise the rent on his folks because it might put them in a financial bind and he felt guilty about raising the rent on them because of their economic circumstances. So, rather than make waves he bit the bullet and subliminally decided he was not going to make money but was going to be a social worker instead.

You see this is a mental and emotional problem for Rick. It's not like he said to himself that he is going to cut these people a break and take a financial hit as a result. This is a mental game that he is dealing with.

Are you laughing at this? Does this sound crazy to you? I know to many of you reading this it will sound bizarre, but I see it all the time.

I not only see it from current owners but from new owners as well.

Picture what these owners do. They do so much work and spend a lot of time and even money finally getting that RIGHT project only to let their guilt stop them from making any money.

They purchase the property and are ready to raise rents. They start the process and then get some of the tenants complaining about it—some with emotion—that their rent is being raised $50 - $100 per month and what are they going to do? They cannot afford that, they say! You are a slumlord they say! You are greedy, they say! So, what do many people do? They crumble to this guilt trip and they either don't raise the rent or they only raise it a little. Now a project that **WAS** going to be very profitable is only marginally profitable (if at all) and now you have set the tone for the duration of your ownership of the property, and have let all of the tenants know that you are a social worker not an investor. I see it all the time.

So, how do you avoid becoming a Social Worker? Easy. First, start by remembering this statement:

THE TENANTS' ECONOMIC CONDITION IS NOT YOUR FAULT OR YOUR PROBLEM. YOU ARE NOT RESPONSIBLE FOR YOUR TENANTS ABUNDANCE OR LACK OF IT.

Whether the tenant has money or not is THEIR problem, not yours. It is neither because of you that they may not be in the best position financially nor because of how much you may raise their rent. You are not responsible for their well being. They are!

The second thing to remember is:

THIS IS BUSINESS. YOUR JOB AS THE OWNER OF THE BUSINESS (PROPERTY) IS TO MAXIMIZE PROFIT OF THE SHAREHOLDERS...PERIOD. WHETHER OR NOT YOU ARE THE SOLE SHAREHOLDER (OWNER) IS OF NO CONSEQUENCE.

You are in this to make money for yourself and/or the people that you care about. Why else would you go through all of this trouble? Again— if you want to HELP people, volunteer or contribute to charity.

The third and final thing to remember is:

EVEN IF THE TENANTS LEAVE, YOU WILL FIND OTHERS THAT WILL GLADLY PAY YOU MUCH HIGHER RENTS ANYWAY. THE CURRENT TENANTS ARE NOT A PERMANENT FIXTURE OF THE PROPERTY AND CANNOT BE TREATED THAT WAY!!

The great news for the tenants is that if they think your rents are too high and it will be too tough to take care of financially, then, they can move! They do not HAVE to stay there and pay the higher rent. In the US, they are free to go other places and pay a rental amount that they can more easily afford! They are not trees permanently rooted to your property.

The other part to this is what you need to do, and your attitude in terms of once some of your tenants do leave. Again, this is where some will get tripped up. They think that the tenants leaving would be bad because then you will have a lot of empty units. Empty units = no income. No income = problems. So, it is EASIER to leave low rent paying tenants there so we do not have a large vacancy and therefore no cash flow problems.

In a word, this kind of thinking is dumb! Remember, if you bought the property using our criteria there is no question you can get residents to move into the units at a higher rent! Also, the more units you have vacant at one time the faster you can get them rented up AT THE HIGHER RENT and the FASTER YOU WILL REACH YOUR FINANCIAL GOALS!

Once you reach your financial goals you can help out as many people as you want. Make sure your apartment property investment is not the area of charity you do this in. If you adopt this attitude or carry this emotional baggage, you could go years and make no profit as a result.

THE EXCEPTION TO ALL OF THIS.

The only exception to everything I have mentioned in this chapter is if you truly do not take care of the property from a maintenance, repair, and providing a decent place for tenants to live standpoint. If you take the stand that you will be bleeding the property dry and not taking care of day to day maintenance items and tenant problems. If you knowingly steal money from the property or its residences through neglect of the property and safety of the residents, then you are a person of little integrity and deserve everything you have coming to you from the residents or others. You can make a lot of money by following our system without known and bold face negligence. Make sure you do not go down that road.

Final Tip.

One way to avoid this emotional hang up altogether is to have a barrier between you and the tenants. In other words I recommend having a property management company in place taking your orders from day 1 of ownership. This way the property managers can deal with the tenants one-on-one and deal with all this baggage, instead of you. It simply takes you out of this emotional equation.

Remember, this is about how you can make more money DOING LESS! Simply put, a good property management company takes all of the emotion out of it for you and takes care of any potential tenant problems by shielding you from any potential problems from tenants or from the property that may influence your decision making. By having a management company in place you are more objective and can make decisions from a business standpoint not an emotional standpoint, another good reason to have a good management company in place.

Remember, this is a business of profit. Helping people have a nice place to live is a byproduct of that. Do not get these two mixed up.

Step 7—invest in the Real Estate For the Right Reasons!!! You are in this to make yourself and any of your partners a profit. Do not use your property as a charity to contribute to those that may be less fortunate than you. That is what charities are for.

SECTION II—WHAT TO DO ONCE YOU HAVE THE INVESTMENT IN YOUR SIGHTS—YOUR PATH TO FAST PROFITS

CHAPTER 9

YOU FOUND THE PROPERTY—THE NUMBERS MEET YOUR CRITERIA...NOW WHAT?

Okay, you or your broker have found the right apartment property. It has passed our litmus test both in terms of location and the income and expense rule of 9%. It looks like THIS ONE COULD BE THE ONE! Now what?

Make an offer on the property.

But wait a minute? Shouldn't I do an inspection first?

No you should not! In fact do not even think about it at this point.

Huh?

Okay, follow me on this. The most important aspect of any apartment project we are going to be looking at buying is what? Is it the brick exterior, the carpet, the paint color?? No! The numbers and the financials that make up the property are what the most important thing here is. So, one of the most important numbers that we need to work on is the sales price isn't it? If we cannot get the project for a price that makes financial sense to us, (in terms of where the rental and expense numbers are now and where they can be) why in the heck waste your time inspecting the property then finding out you can't get it for the price you need? Doesn't make sense, so, lets start by making an offer on the property—it cuts to the chase and saves us a lot of precious time.

Your Three Steps to A Great 'Locked In Profit' Purchase Price.

More than likely if the property meets our criteria, most of the time we can 'live' with the asking price. Now, I did not say we pay the asking price but part of the property passing our litmus test remember is that once we factor in REALISTICALLY how much the property will be worth when we are done with it the asking price should be in the ballpark of making sense. However, we sure don't want to pay the asking price of the property. The ONLY time you even consider doing that is IF it is REALLY a winner at the asking price.

So, here is what you would typically do….

Set the three prices you are willing to pay for the property. Here is how you do it.

1st Price: Dream Price to Purchase.
2nd Price: Great Price to Purchase.
3rd Price: Price You Can Live With.

Okay, let's use an example. Say the asking price on an apartment property is $750,000. After you do your homework you find it passes our litmus test and it would be a good project to pick up—even at $750,000. But again, we want to make not just a little money but a lot so our interest in this is going to be to pay less than asking price. No huge revelation here.

BEFORE YOU MAKE ANY OFFER ON ANY PROPERTY!

You FIRST do the math and figure your dream price. Let's say in this example it would be $640,000. This would be a price where you would for sure hit that home run. So, your initial offer is $640,000. The Dream Price.

You then take a look at the project in terms of what your second offer will be. Based on the numbers if the seller does not accept your offering price of $640,000 you will come in at $693,000. Remember this is our Great Price. Then lastly, in the event the seller does not take your second offer of $693,000 you establish the third and final offer price of $730,000—This is our Can Live with It price.

Remember, these figures are based on what you feel is the best prices for you to buy the property. Again you go from dream price paid to more than acceptable price paid with your range.

So, your offer sequence will be:

1. Offer 1 - $640,000. If not accepted....
2. Offer 2 - $693,000. If not accepted...
3. Offer 3 - $730,000. Final offer.

Now of course if you get the seller to counter offer at a price LESS than any of these in this example that is a GOOD THING! For example if you make your first offer at $640,000 and then the seller comes back at $690,000 you work on getting that down as low as you can because you know you are already going to get the price LESS THAN YOUR GREAT PRICE CEILING.

Another example. Say you offer $640,000 and the seller counters at $727,000. You go with offer 2 of $693,000 and then the seller counters at $719,000. This is GOOD NEWS SINCE ARE WORKING ON A PRICE THAT IS LESS THAN THE TOP DOLLAR YOU WOULD BE WILLING TO PAY...IN THIS EXAMPLE $730,000. Now your job is to work that $719,000 counter offer as low as you can. You get the picture by now.

Why do I prefer this method? Because you have already set parameters on the price you will pay for a property BEFORE you start your negotiation not DURING the negotiation. You want the math to be already worked out in your head and on paper before you start. You do not want to do this on the fly. It's akin to going to a real estate auction (or any auction for that matter) and establishing the top price you are going to pay for a property, and not go over that price no matter what happens during the bidding process. Same is true here.

Any time you can get the property for less than really any price you have 'pre-established' you will have a winner on your hands. Again, you have already identified the property as a winner—now it is taking the next step and making the property a champion and by using this method of negotiating price will take the property from a winner to a champion.

A Shortcut to Profitable Properties

What type of current apartment owner is the best candidate to be leasing their units for too little by not paying attention to market rent and paying too much in expenses??

1. Out of town owners.
2. Long term, older Free and Clear owners.

Most of the great projects that I have purchased and made a good amount of money on have been from the above two categories.

Out of town owners. Many out of town owners have no clue where the market rent needs to be and what they need to do in order to increase their income and reduce their expenses. To their detriment they depend on a management company to do that for them. BAD DECISION. Why? The management company is in the business and their staff are trained to do one thing…Manage the Day to Day Operations of the property. They are NOT trained to make the property cash flow better! Simply put they are trained and excel at babysitting not at money making. Never forget this!

However, there are a lot of owners that depend on their management company to keep the rent at market levels and expenses at a minimum; and this spells opportunity. The thing to keep in mind here is that usually the time the owners find out that they have been missing out on more cash flow is when they are ready to sell. The good news for us is that they usually do not change their mind and say, "Okay, let's forget about selling for 12 months until we can get the rents changed and the expenses in line." - Nope—that usually does not happen because when an owner decides that they want or NEED to sell they do not have the ability to wait 12 months to get it done—not to mention the transition problems that will result in a major property change. So, in most cases they have to sell the property in its existing "rent" condition. Again, good news for us!

Now, keep in mind that about 60% of these out of town owners—even at the point of selling their property—do not know that they have a problem and sell the property at a huge discount…and not even know it. Again, good news for us.

Long Term Owners and Free and Clear Owners.

I can think back, right now, of three scenarios in just the last few months where we bought a project owned by someone that had owned it for 25+ years OR owned the property Free and Clear. Many long term owners lose focus toward the end of their 'apartment investment life' and do not stay on top of the property like they should. If they get a decent check once a month for the cash flow and they are not making any waves with the tenants then they think this is a good thing—even if the property is not operating at it fullest capacity because there is no debt to service any longer. They get nice large monthly checks but in turn lose focus on how much rent they should be getting.

Same goes for the Free and Clear owners. Again, as long as they are getting a nice check once a month they are happy and do not want to rock the boat.

In a sense, for the Free and Clear owners and the Long Term Owners IT BECOMES ABOUT PRESERVING THE CURRENT CASH FLOW VS. GROWING IT. They start to get conservative and play to not lose any money vs. play to win, if you follow me.

Again—ALL of this means nice future profits for you.

I realize that sometimes it sounds hard to believe that an owner is not up to snuff on his rents and on keeping his expenses down. Keep in mind that this is pretty much the same way a business is run. There are many businesses that perform OK but do not perform as well as they should simply because of the owner and their philosophies, hiring practices, attitudes, etc. keeps them from maximizing the amount of money the property can and in many cases will easily produce.

Step 8–You now have the means to not only locate but negotiate the best deal that will virtually guarantee you profits at the closing table! You are well on your way! For more assistance in getting the best price on a project you can download the Apartment Offer and Acceptance Worksheet at www.9monthinvestment.com. Also remember, some of the best deals will come from out of town owners and owners who have property with no debt! It's always worth asking if there is any underlying loans that can be assumed because that tells you if there is any debt on the property or not.

Chapter 10

Where To Find the Capital To Do This

Remember, our goal is to simply purchase a well located apartment building using the rules and strategies we discussed earlier and make a lot of money from doing so in a 9 month period. So, the question becomes where should the capital come from to invest in the property in the first place? Where do I find it?

Or said another way, "I found the property that will make a lot of money....Now what?"

In this chapter I am going to discuss various ways to use your capital or in some cases, other peoples capital to make this work for you. Lets start with the easy items and then move up to a bit more sophisticated. You may of course use one or a combination of ways to put capital in your property...

The key thing to remember here is what I call safe leverage. I recommend investing as much as you can comfortably into the apartment property but not all of your spare change and use the power of borrowing money to fill in the gaps. For example, if the property is $500,000 and you have $200,000 you can comfortably put into that project that is great. Now your job is to borrow the remaining $300,000 from the bank or from the seller. However, if you can come up with say $50,000 then you can still do this, however, now you will have to find out where to come up with the remaining $450,000. You get the picture. A key thing to understand is that your large increase in value will happen no matter if you put $200,000 or $50,000 into the property. For example:

Apartment Purchase Price: $500,000
Value In 9 Months: $700,000
Profit: $200,000.

If I invested $200,000 of my capital I have basically doubled my money haven't I? I will get $400,000 out of the property from my original investment of $200,000 PLUS the $200,000 in profits for a total of $400,000. This is the power of leverage.

Now, imagine if I put $50,000 into the property but it appreciated to $700,000 in 9 months. I get $250,000 back from my $50,000 investment! That is huge! Again, the power of leverage.

Do you see where doing just a few of these every year can make you wealthy?

One caution. Many so-called experts want you to almost always use as little of your own cash to do this as possible and why not—it gives you the best return doesn't it? Even though the numbers are impressive when you do this, I do not necessarily always agree. I think you should be investing as much of your own capital as you comfortably can, so the amount you borrow from the bank or the seller is at least 70% or less of the purchase price of the property. I like to have some room in there and not borrow too much just in case it takes longer to get the property turned around or there is an unforeseen problem that crops up. The items that can surprise you that could cost you money along the way will not be so bad IF you have plenty of equity invested in the property. Its when you over leverage and borrow to the hilt is when you can make large profits but also can have large problems as well.

Remember my rule of 70%.

With that in mind, let's talk about other places we can find investment dollars to go into our next apartment project:

Cash, Savings, CD's, Money Market Funds, Etc.

This is probably the easiest place to find cash to put into your projects. I call this basically the cookie jar. Many people have money sitting in savings accounts or bank certificates of deposit. Many times the interest being earned on these accounts is not very good. A great way to improve these account balances is to find that right apartment property.

Mutual Funds, Stocks.

This is another good source for funding your acquisition, in mutual funds or stocks. Many people can be hesitant about this because either they may take a loss OR they may take a nice profit and have to pay taxes on the profit. All of this does not matter. Why? Because the amount of money that you will make from using your funds to invest in well located apartment properties will more than offset any taxes you would have to pay or any loss you may have to incur in order to sell your stocks or mutual funds.

IRA/401 K/ROTH IRA/Company Retirement Plans

Did you know that you can use your retirement accounts for this? The fact is you can have these kinds of profits we have been talking about in this book tax deferred! Imagine using your IRA to invest $100,000 into an apartment property and once you are done with it you sell the property and profit $250,000. That $150,000 profit goes right into your IRA account—tax deferred. Many of my clients do just this. I believe this concept is so important that I have devoted an entire chapter to this, later in this book.

Forming A Simple Partnership And Using An LLC.

You can also bring in some partners to fill in any gaps. The bottom line is the larger the property you purchase the larger the profits right? There may be a property that is going to require more of a cash investment into it that you have OR that you feel comfortable making. A solution may be to get in touch with a few friends or relatives and form a partnership to purchase the property. The majority of the apartment properties that I have been involved in have been partnerships with other like-minded investors.

Partnerships have been a very valuable tool for me and for my partners. It allows me to invest in much larger properties thereby, my profits are much larger AND it allows my partners to profit as well; and they have no work, time or effort involved in the property. They are simply along for the ride and profiting from it as well.

Partnerships are not that difficult to put together or manage as long as you remember a couple of key points:

1. Make Sure **You** are the manager of the partnership and are running the show. Do not let anyone else run the investment—especially someone that has no idea about this BUT think they do and/or are not even there. For example, with my partnerships I run the show on all of them and make the majority of decisions. Kind of like a general contractor in a way. If it is an important issue, such as replacing a roof for example, I will advise my partners and ask for feedback. But, if I am working on increasing the income and reducing the expenses on the property with the daily decisions that need to be made, then I have the authority to handle that. This will need to be known by everyone up front. You cannot run a successful partnership by committee on every single item. Most of your partners will actually agree with this and not want to be in on those decisions anyway. However, if you have someone that wants to get their fingers involved in every facet of the process for the privilege of being your partner, my recommendation is to NOT accept them and kindly tell them to move on or that you are full.

2. Use an LLC for your partnership. Most of the time you will want to use a Limited Liability Company as umbrella or entity for your partnership. You will of course want to run this by your attorney but I can tell you with a great deal of confidence that this will more than likely be the case for most. An LLC or Limited Liability Company is simply a legal entity that you and your partners will form together as the owner of the property, but it will also serve as the 'rules and regulations' of your partnership as well as outline the responsibilities of each of your partners. Once you and your partners become members of your newly formed LLC then it will be the LLC that will be the buyer/investor in the property that you are going to purchase. A partners' ownership interest in the LLC is usually based on the amount of capital the partner contributes.

For example. Let's say that you find a $1,000,000 property. You have done the homework and think it could be a $1,500,000 property in about 12 months time. Knowing the rule of 70% you know you can borrow $700,000 to purchase the property and now you need to come up with the remaining $300,000.

Let's say you have $150,000 of your own capital to put into the property. Now you need an additional $150,000 to get to your $300,000 investment.

You contact two people that you know would have an interest in this and both say they are IN for $75,000 each. Here is how it looks at this point:

You - $150,000
Partner 1 - $75,000
Partner 2 - $75,000

All three of you meet and decide to move forward on the property. At that time you decide to form an LLC to purchase the property with the three of you being the members of the LLC and YOU being the managing member of that LLC. Everyone's ownership interest in the LLC is computed as follows:

Total Investment: $300,000

Your Investment: $150,000	50%
Partner 1 Investment: $75,000	25%
Partner 2 Investment: $75,000	25%
	100%

So what this means is YOU will have a 50% ownership in the LLC and your partners will each have 25% ownership in the LLC. In general, your ownership in the LLC will be based on each person's total capital contribution into the LLC divided by the total capital contributions of all partners as you see above.

Now, what happens when you actually purchase the property is your new LLC will actually purchase the property. All of the benefits of the property purchase will then be based on each person's ownership interest in the LLC. In other words, your percentage of benefit from the property will be based on your ownership interest in the LLC.

As I mentioned earlier in the chapter, a large amount of property that I own is in an LLC partnership like I just described. You will find many people that would love to be involved in a great apartment investment but do not have the time nor desire to figure all of this out themselves and would be happy to have you DO IT FOR THEM and be your partner.

For examples on the partnership agreements for LLC's that I use as well as my rules and guidelines for running a successful partnership you can go to www.9monthinvestment.com and get your examples.

Your Best Course Of Action

Many times your best course of action on a great apartment property is to use a combination of all of the above. Not only can you use a combination of all of the items in this chapter, but keep in mind that any of your partners can do the same thing and they may have money in their retirement account, etc. that would be very good for this. I have many projects that have retirement money in them, and some regular money as well as partner money. Always remember, the fastest way to your wealth goals is by doing as much as possible all at once vs. one thing at a time!

Again, this is where a good attorney, accountant, as well as a real estate broker can assist you and make this an easy process. You can have all of these items going on at one time and with your strong supporting cast you will be able to accomplish more in less time.

Step 9–involves coming up with your investment dollars to put into the 9-month investment. The best bet is to use a combination of ideas in this chapter. For more ideas and even partnership agreements you can go to www.9monthinvestment.com.

CHAPTER 11

YOU HAVE FOUND IT, NOW HOW DO YOU FINANCE IT?

You have done a good job of doing your work to find that 9 month investment and using the system that I have outlined for you in this book. You have talked to lenders, appraisers and brokers. You have actually gone out and taken a look at a few properties and maybe tried to invest in a couple. You have taken some swings at a property.

But after a few weeks or months of work on this you have finally found THE property, put it through our litmus test, taken it through our system and want to invest in it. It is going to be a real winner for you! Now you just have to get the property purchased.

But now what? You found it and you are ready to move forward on it but the asking price on the property is $900,000. You think this can be worth $1,400,000 in the next 9 months and you only have $200,000 to put into the property. Where are you going to get the other $700,000??

This will be subject matter of this chapter, basically, where do you come up with what I call "THE REST". You know, the difference between the price of the property and the amount of money you want (or in most cases HAVE) to invest in it? Where do you come up with "THE REST?"

I will give you some methods of financing the property you want to invest in, coming up with 'THE REST' starting with the easiest method and then getting on to the more complicated. One of these methods should work for you. You can find more information on great financing techniques at www.9monthinvestment.com.

Remember we want to have our business plan for the property done first and we covered how to do that and where to get that in previous chapters. Not only is this good for US to have, it is good for the lender to have as well, so they can see what it is that you are doing and can feel more 'bankable' about you too.

Here are the methods for getting your project financed:

Conventional Bank Financing.

This is the easiest way to go. Banks and Credit Unions will lend on apartment properties. Their criteria is that they will usually lend up to 75–80% of the purchase price or appraised value—whichever is less. So, in our example of a $900,000 purchase, they will lend you from $675,000 - $720,000. You will need to come up with the rest.

At this point many people get down because they have to come up with around $200,000. However I have the opposite view. I can buy a $1,400,000 asset for $900,000 with $200,000! Now to me THAT IS A DEAL!

Sometimes you may be successful in having a lender loan you a bit more than the 75% - 80% if you show them your business plan of where you will be taking the value up and up and how you will be getting there. Many times I have been able to get the lender to loan me more than they typically do because of what they see I will be doing. Now, this does not work all of the time but it is something to try for.

You should have a nice short list of aggressive lenders to contact and to get your financing based on the calls you were making in earlier chapters. Armed with the right lenders, a great property and a completed business plan for that property, you are ready to roll. This should be pretty easy.

The only thing to really be aware about the local banks and credit unions is that they will require a lot of information from you. They will want copies of your tax returns and a copy of your current financial statement too. Don't get too stressed out about this since this is par for the course and not out of the ordinary. The property information they can get and will get from your business plan.

Now the lender will take the following information:

1. Your (and/or any partners that will join you) tax returns for last two years.
2. Your (and/or any partners that will join you) current *financial statement.
3. Current Property Description.
4. Current Property Cash Flow
5. Your business plan.

*If you need a blank financial statement to fill out for your lenders simply go to <u>www.9monthinvestment.com</u> and click on the Resources Tab and download it. Not only is this good to have for your lenders but it is a great measuring stick for you to keep track of your personal wealth!

What the lender will now do is see IF they want to finance this for you. This is why it is important to have more than one lender looking at a project at any given time since some lenders will really like it, some not so much. You can have the same information on the same property and one lender may fall in love with it and another may run away just as fast. So, use more than one lender.

Again, after the lender looks at the information they will decide if it is something they want to finance. If it is not a project they want to finance they will tell you as much. Thank them and move on. DO NOT get angry, upset or take it personally—this is business not your personal life.

If the lender decides it is something that they may want to finance then they will get you a term sheet that outlines how much money they will lend you, what interest rate, what the cost of the loan will be and what is expected of you and the property in order to get this loan. Again, this is called a TERM SHEET.

The goal for you is to get as many Term Sheets as you can, so you can compare lenders and then work with the one that will be the most aggressive in terms of interest rate, up front fees and what they will demand over the life of the loan. Of course go with the lender that is going to give you the best rate and terms based on what you plan on doing with the property.

If you are investing IRA money into the property you want to make sure there is nothing on the Term Sheet about a personal guarantee. See the Advanced IRA investment strategies section for more information.

One quick note here. Many people do not want to approach lenders because of the hassle it may entail or maybe they had a bad experience before. Do not let this get in your way. One thing that has really helped me get deals done is my relationship with lenders. Having this relationship has helped me a lot in terms of what I have been able to purchase for me and my partners—especially if they are, really trusting my gut on a property. Make sure you do not overlook this.

Owner Financing.

One of my favorite methods of buying apartments is using owner financing. When you use owner financing you do not have to go through the majority of hassles as you would with a bank, it costs you less in fees and you can get the deal done much faster with usually no prepayment penalties. Many times with owner financing, you will not have to sign a personal guarantee nor will you need to prove you or your partners' financial worth and it's a lot less hassle. If you can do it, always try to get the project financed by the owner first.

Owner financing is really easy. Bottom line is the owner, not the bank, is lending you the money to purchase. Here is how a typical deal would work:

Let's say you spot a property for $2,000,000. You think in the next 9 months this can be a $2,700,000 property but you have to come up with $2,000,000 to start working on this. What you do, is offer the owner a down payment of $300,000 and the balance of $1,700,000 to be financed by him or her at an agreed upon interest rate and repayment term. So, what you do is you pay the owner $300,000 down payment at closing and the owner carries you on the remaining $1,700,000 at an agreed upon interest rate, term and monthly payment. That is how you get to the $2,000,000.

Pretty simple huh?

All with no bank! Remember, this way is easier and less expensive also.

So, why would an owner go this route instead of wanting to get all of their money in cash from the sale? There are many reasons why an owner would do this....

A) Property sells faster.
B) Get a price usually closer to asking price.
C) Can defer paying taxes. With owner financing the owner pays taxes as they receive the money.
D) Get a nice predictable monthly income.
E) Get a nice return on the amount being financed.
F) Gets monthly cash flow without having to deal with any management.

I not only gave you this information because I thought it was a good idea but also because of what you need to know to work on an owner that has maybe not thought about this before. These are just a few reasons and you may need to educate the seller on some of these or at least tactfully bring them up IF the seller balks at any owner financing options. The point is, make sure you ask and ask again on this.

Partners.

One of the most utilized strategies that I have used over the years is partners. There are many reasons to bring in partners but for now, lets focus on the financing part of things. I am going to divide this into to two parts.

Part A) Down Payment Financing.

Part B) Loan To Purchase The Property Financing.

Let's start with the down payment financing first.

Again, let's use an example. Let's say we are looking at purchasing a property for $900,000. You think this can be a $1,400,000 property in the next 10 months. The owner will consider owner financing but wants a down payment of $350,000. The deal is a good one so you consider how you will get this done BUT the problem is you only have $200,000 to use for the down payment on the property and still need to come up with another $150,000.

Where do you get the other $150,000 for down payment? A partner or partners, that is where…

Believe me when I tell you there are A LOT of people that would love to partner with you on a deal like this—especially when they have not had to do the work or spend the time finding a deal like this. For them to own a percentage interest in the property especially with the potential profits you are looking at will get people interested—believe me.

The simplest way to describe this process would be you put your $200,000 in the kitty, your partner(s) then puts in their $150,000. You now have $350,000 to move forward on the property! Based on these numbers you would have an ownership interest of 57% and your partner has an interest of 43%.

This is a great way to own larger properties that you would not be able to otherwise. Just think of it this way. Would you rather have a $2,000,000 property appreciate 10% or $200,000 OR would you rather have a $200,000 property appreciate 10% or $2,000? Of course, both returns are of the same rate but with one property I got $200,000 coming to me and the other I have only 1/10th that…$20,000. Again, this is using leverage at its best, so a partnership situation could work very, very well.

Another Option….

The second way, partner for the loan on the property instead of the down payment can work for you too. In addition to finding a partner to invest with you in that down payment, you can ALSO find partners that want to BE THE BANK and have large ownerships in the property. Many people, as I describe in my **7 figures in 7 Weeks** system http://www.myplatinumclub.com/products/item16.cfm have a lot of cash sitting in money markets, savings accounts, CD's. They are looking for higher rates of return but they are conservative. Many would consider being the bank on your property since they will get a nice return on their money and be in a safe position from an equity and property value standpoint.

For example—I just bought an 8 unit property for $322,000. The loan amount on this property was $200,000. I had a client of mine that wanted to become a partner and take on that $200,000 so it was essentially an all cash transaction. I and one partner put in the down payment - $122,000—the other partner put up the $200,000 in a loan to us. Total–$322,000.

So you can have a partner(s) for the down payment, for the loan or both!

This kind of process reminds me of something else and I need to tell you about this....

Private Lenders.

Private lending is sort of a partnership like we just described except there are a couple of key differences. One is that you are looking for someone, other than a bank, finance company or loan shark to loan you money to purchase the property—period. This loan could be for the down payment OR for the majority amount needing financed or both.

A private lender is a private party, who would typically be someone that wants a good return on their money and not connected with any kind of bank or lending institution. Where as a partnership wants to own the property and grow it and make it more valuable and own it as profitably as possible the private lender just wants a return on their money backed by the property as collateral and by you and does not want to own or manage anything. They just want cash flow and return.

Of course, the Private lender will want to know about your plans to make the property more valuable and how you plan on making your profit, etc. but they will want to get maximum return for investing more in the property than you are. That is right, keep in mind that if a Private lender loans you say 60% of the purchase price of a property they are really investing more than you in the property aren't they??

So really, they are investors just like you but with a slight twist.

Types of Private Lending—What To Expect.

There are no rules for private lending. Bottom line is you get what you negotiate because there really are no guidelines, however, over time there are some consistencies that you can use. Let me tell you what you want and what your private lender will want:

YOU will want the longest term loan at the lowest interest rate at the lowest cost possible. The private lender? Will want the shortest term loan with the highest interest at the highest cost. Wow, what a surprise huh?

So, when you start talking to a private lender map out what you are willing to accept and deal with at the outset. Get in idea, worst case, what you would settle for and stick to your guns. Approach a private lending opportunity the same way you did with making an offer on the property. Have a best case scenario, good scenario and worst case scenario in mind BEFORE you start your negotiating. Of course, most private lenders will have an idea as to what is acceptable to them and will communicate that to you at the outset.

Who Are Private Lenders?

Like potential partners, private lenders are either 'mom and pop' people wanting to make a nice return on their investment all the way to the person that pools money together from individuals and makes loans on behalf of these individuals. So, you will have folks just in this on a couple of deals all the way to people doing this for a substantial part of their income. It will be all over the map in terms of whom you may end up working with.

In its simplest form, a private lender could be your Uncle Phil loaning you money to purchase that 8 unit apartment property all the way to

Smith and Jones Company from a big office tower in a big city loaning you money to buy that 80 unit property.

Again, you could go from one extreme to the other.

Why Use Private Lenders and what to Expect.

Of course, the main reason to use a private lender is the hassle factor. A private lender typically will not require the same kind of criteria or underwriting that a bank does—especially if they are familiar with you. Most private lenders are simply looking for a good return on their money with little risk. I will get more into dealing with the perceived risk of a property very soon but the best private lenders for you to work with are those that know you and or know of you and are comfortable with your process of working the 9 month investment system and lastly, are comfortable with the property.

Of course a private lender may still want an appraisal on the property from an independent third party and may also want comment from that third party on your business plan so be prepared.

When it comes to private lenders, the closer they are to you and the more that they trust in what you are doing, the less information you will have to present in order for them to be "IN" on any deal that you are doing. The further away you get from an already existing relationship with a private lender the more information they will want about you and your property and the more scrutiny you will face.

Entice Them With Ownership As Well??

One of the rabbits you may want to pull out of your hat if:

1. You have a private lender really close on your deal but not quite there—say—90% there but there may be a small reason they choose not to move forward. OR...
2. You have a great project that will be making you a nice large profit and you are fairly certain of this in a reasonable period of time—say 6 months.

Then you may want to keep your costs down by offering them an ownership in the property IN ADDITION TO having them loan you money.

There are many different ways of doing this and you can come up with 200 arrangements if you wanted. Let me give you a couple of examples first.

A) You have an 84 unit property that can be purchased for $4,000,000. You believe this can be a $5,000,000 deal once you take it through the 9 month system. Problem is, you can only come up with $350,000 down payment and $1,000,000 is required. What do you do?

Find a private lender to loan you the remaining $650,000 in down payment loan. Rather than paying the lender a high interest rate on this loan of say 14% why not pay them 9% but give them a 5% ownership in the property? Not only will the private lender get a nice 9% return they will also get a nice chunk of the profits from the property—in this case $50,000! This may be enough of an argument to get the private lender who was on the fence to fully commit to the project.

B) Another example. Let's use the same example. You have the $1,000,000 down payment but you cannot find any traditional lenders to work with you for whatever reason. You need another $3,000,000 and are looking for a loan. What to do?!

Offer a private lender a 10% ownership in the property and an 8% return until the property is sold or refinanced. You would pay $240,000 of interest on the loan (if you went annual or 12 months) and when the property sold you would pay them an additional $100,000 in profits from the sale from having a 10% ownership interest in the property. Total over a one year period of time here is $340,000 to your private lender. Quite a nice profit for them!

But wait! You profited too! Remember, you put $1,000,000 into this property didn't you? Once the dust settles—even after one year you are getting over $600,000 in profits on your $1,000,000 investment. This is a 60% return. Does not take you long to shrink ordinary time to grow your investments when you get 60% returns!!

Remember you ONLY want to use this strategy IF your property has enough profits coming and as a last straw but many times this can be convincing to investors, especially when they are hands off. You also want to be conservative with your numbers and your time frames for getting the project completed.

Finding Private Lenders

There are three main ways to find private lenders: 1) Advertise. 2) Word of Mouth or Leverage of Relationships. 3) Marketing to Predisposed Leads.

Let's start with Advertising:

I just ran across an ad on Craiglist.com from a guy looking for capital to fund his apartment purchase. Here is what it said.

Need $400,000 JV on an apartment complex now at 40% occupancy. Will be 95% occupied in 12 months or less. Great location and area— property was badly mismanaged. For details email frank@frank.com

This is an example of someone advertising for a private lender. You will see these kinds of ads in national venues like Craigslist, Wall Street Journal, Investors Business Daily, etc. You can even do this in your local newspaper or on your local online hot spots.

There are always investors looking for places to put their money. No matter what the economy is doing! Don't forget that. In the 'Capital Wanted' or 'Joint Ventures' or 'Money To Invest' sections of papers and internet sites you will find people advertising here. This is an easy place to start. Depending on the size and the profits of your project will really tell you where you should go. Of course the larger the property and the larger the profits the more you can afford to spend and the more sites or publications you can afford and should be in.

Here is an example that I would use:

Large Predictable Profits and Cash Flow

Have a 72 unit apartment property that will produce REALISTIC predictable cash flows and large profits in the near term. Ready to go on turning this project around.

Have business plan for review. Property location, profits and track record reveal a real winner here—will not last long. For your free business plan on the project and detailed information call 333-33-3333 or email frank@frank.com.

This is the kind of ad that can be placed in either a local or national publication. The national publications that I recommend are the Wall Street Journal and Investors Business Daily. Your business plan that you can share with them you can get from my web site at www.9monthinvestment.com as well as an example of this ad for you to use and copy if you want.

The good news and the bad news is that the larger the readership the more response you will get. I say good news and bad news because bottom line is you get what you pay for. So, if you want big numbers you will be paying for national publications and that will run much more in money than local marketing. Local marketing will of course save you on costs but it will not give you large numbers.

Again, we don't necessarily need large numbers for us to achieve our goals but the larger the pond to fish from that contains more fish—the better.

Where To Test Your Ads For Private Money

Now regarding this, it makes sense to test locally first but whatever you do, DO NOT discount national investors wanting to be in on your deals—there are more national investors that will have an interest than local. Sounds a bit odd but true. My own experience has taught me that there is demand for what you have more nationally than locally—in terms of numbers of people interested in my deals. However, the national media costs about 10 times more than the local media does. IF you can afford it though, make sure you do test national media as well but try to test an ad that you feel comfortable will work.

Remember print media is good but I have also tested and used successfully internet sites such as Craigslist, www.ebay.com and www.loopnet.com and I am sure there are others.

A last thought on this kind of advertising is, if you can afford to do it, I would do it in a place on a regular basis not just when a deal comes up. For example, if I have an ad that when ran produced a nice amount of leads I would continue to run that ad even if you do not have a deal 'in the hopper' yet. Then, when people respond and if the project was already completed or is 'in process', then I would tell the people such but suggest that they stay on my list to be contacted for the next similar deal that may come up and get their contact information. This way you are continuously collecting a bank of leads that you can take your next deal to that are already interested vs. starting the placing the ad process all over again. This will save you a lot of time and money in the long run.

Word of Mouth / Leverage Relationships To Get Your Private Money

As you have probably guessed, this is basically using the people you already know or already have a relationship with to be your partner or private lender. This would include friends, relatives, business associates, co-workers, etc. It is the old exercise of sitting down and writing out 100 people that you know and then going to them for Private Money. This also works if you are looking for partners as well. It is really about relationships and who you have them with.

CAUTION. Make sure that if you go into business with someone you know that they pass the "If I do business with this person, is it going to be more of a hassle and potential problems than it is worth" Test. Here is what I mean.

There are people (and you KNOW who they are) that would be a huge pain in the rear and a huge problem. Yes, they may be able to come up with cash to be a Private Lender but the amount of maintenance and work these people would need and cause you would not be worth it. By the way, I am speaking to you about this from real experience.

For example, I had a neighbor of mine some years back tell me that he would have an interest in partnering with me on my next project. Nice guy but from what I knew of him and knew of his personality that he would be a huge problem in terms of day to day 'maintenance'. Against my better judgment I let him in on my next project. Bad decision. From the very beginning he was questioning me on every decision related to the property, wanted to be kept up to date almost daily with progress reports to him personally and even suggested that I change accountants because the one I had used for 10 years was one day behind in getting us some required information. He also wanted to have about one face to face meeting on the property once every two weeks and this guy was a small minority private lender.

I think you get the point here. You will know, instinctively, the people that will cause you headaches and problems. You will also be tempted to have them as your private lender (or partner) because you think you may "need" them. Let me just tell you from experience it is just not worth it. Trust me on this. Follow your gut—even if they have the money to go into your deals.

Now onto my favorite—Getting in touch with predisposed leads.

You know, I love the word predisposed. In the real estate world that we occupy this word means THE PEOPLE WHO, MORE THAN ANY OTHER, WANT TO DO BUSINESS WITH US AS OUR PRIVATE FUNDING SOURCE/PARTNER. So, let me ask you, when it comes to real estate projects—specifically commercial real estate projects, who is more likely to have an interest in working, funding or partnering with us? A

1. Nurse.
2. Doctor.
3. A School Teacher.
4. An Owner of Commercial Real Estate
5. A Factory Worker.

If you said #4 you were right on! The others COULD be interested in being our private funding source or partners with us BUT more than likely CHANCES ARE, the owner of a commercial real estate property is more apt to be in that position. So, who should we be spending our time and attention on first? That is correct the owner of apartments or commercial investment real estate. Why? They understand what you are doing and how you are doing it more than anyone else could— because they have been there.

So, how do you get in touch with these people? Actually, it is pretty easy.

What I recommend is putting together a brief form letter about the project that you are working on. I would send this letter to this 'targeted' group of people talking about your project and its benefits. It is really as simple as that. Type a letter, get a mailing list, use postage, mail and wait for results. Sound easy?

Well, it won't be THAT easy but this is exactly the system that you will follow. What I will do now is give you much more details about how to go about it.

1. Find your next great project that fits our criteria. We have already covered how you find that project and how to take it though our 9 month system.

2. Once you have it put together a 1–3 page letter describing the benefits of the project. When you put the letter together you want to use the 'problem, agitate, solve' formula. Basically, here is how this works: Your first 1/3 part of your letter describes the 'problem' that apartment or commercial property owners' face. Let's say its great cash flow but at a cost of intense and nagging tiring management. Then the next 1/3 of the letter agitates this problem. So, now you talk about what a drain on your time management is and how it can even end up costing them money in the long run or be dangerous at times, etc. Then the last 1/3 letter talks about how your property will solve this problem. I have a template of a letter that I use successfully using the 'Problem, Agitate, Solve' formula at www.9monthinvestment. com that you can download and use for free.

3. Once your letter is done, you obtain the mailing list of apartment and commercial property owners in your area. This should be pretty easy. Simply contact your local title company and they should be able to help you. If for some reason they cannot, then the next best place is your city's tax assessor. They will have apartments and commercial property owners in separate categories and should be able to come up with a list pretty quick. Worst case is they will show you a computer so you can get the names and addresses of the owners yourself.

4. You send out the letter. Now, make sure you follow me here because it will make a difference. Once you send the letter out to the apartment property or commercial property owners in your area you WILL get a response. That's great. Now for a reality check. You will not have 50 out of 100 owners responding to you. As a matter of fact, you may have as low as a 1% response! Now, before you get too discouraged about it, remember we do NOT need big numbers. Just a few of these will work for us. So, your numbers will NOT go through the roof in terms of number of these owners that respond BUT it is important to remember we do NOT need a huge response.

5. After you get your responses you follow up with them and describe your project and see how many you can join you as a Private Lender (make sure you see the takeaway selling information elsewhere in the book).

Now, so far you have made some pretty good progress haven't you? Yes you have, but do we stop here? No. Let me tell you what I am talking about.

How many times have you received something in the mail and you were interested but you had a lot going on at the time. So, what you did was you either filed it or put it in a pile to get to later. Only...you did not get to it later, did you? The daily cares of life got in your way and eventually you threw it away.

I am sure that you can relate to the last paragraph, but what does it have to do with what we are talking about here? It has to do with the awesome four letter word: STEP! That is right—STEP! Now we go to our SECOND STEP of our mailing to our list. Yep, we are going to mail to them again AND we are going to mail to them 10 days after they have received their first mailing.

Why? Because of what I just talked about.

Remember, a rule of thumb is that you will get about half as many responses on the second mailing as you did the first. So, if you mail out this letter the first time and get 20 responses—the second time you mail this you will get around 10 responses.

Now, just think if you did not mail to them again and only mailed to them one time. You would leave 10 responses on the table wouldn't you! One of these responses could be exactly what you need in terms of capital! So, not surprisingly, our next step would be:

6. Send them the same letter as the first letter except put a yellow sticky note on the front page of the letter with the words "second notice" on it. That is right. You send the exact same letter but this time you put a sticky note on it with the words "second notice" on it!

Then of course you would follow-up with those folks that responded as well.

Earlier, I said that you do not need big numbers. That is true, however, if you can get more response that is the best thing isn't it?

7. Once you have hit your group in the mail a couple of times you CAN go for a third time with a letter stating "3rd Notice" and you will get a few more responses. That is correct; you will still get people coming in from this. As crazy as it sounds, it will happen. Of course, once those leads come in you do follow up with them at that time as well.

You see, it is just a matter of sending, see the results and follow-up with those that have responded to you. Of course, remember our realistic measure for how well we are doing. It does not take a lot of responses for us to make money here, so always keep that in mind and don't forget that multi-step process of hitting those people with two or three letters in a 30-day period will work.

Lastly, in order to get as many people interested in being your private money investor you want to do all of these things at the same time! The direct mail campaign, the social networking, and the advertising. If you are looking at getting as many people as possible interested in being a source of private capital for you, then having all of these doors open at once is a great idea and my recommendation on which way you need to go.

There is a difference however in interest on their part; to them actually getting them to give you (lend) their money. I will cover this in the next chapter.

> **Step 10**—Use the systems in this chapter to locate private lenders and partners that are eager to give you their money and invest in your next real estate project. Use social networking, word of mouth, and active marketing. The key to speed and getting this to pay off the fastest for you will be if you do all of this at once. If you commit to this system for over 12 months you will never have to find another partner or private lender "cold" again. There are resources for you to use on the web site at www.9monthinvestment.com.

CHAPTER 12

FINANCING YOUR PROJECT—GETTING FUNDING FROM CONVENTIONAL SOURCES TO COMPLETE THE TASK.

In this chapter, I will not spend a lot of time lecturing to you that you need to work on getting the right loan at the lowest rate at the lowest possible cost with the most flexible terms to take advantage of our 9-month investment. Hello? I think we all know that, that is what you need to do when it comes to getting financing.

So, in this chapter I will tell you the kind of financing you should look for. What you should expect and what you should avoid. There are some key strategies here that I think can make or save you tens of thousands of dollars.

Again, remember that I have no problem in putting as little amount of money in down payment on properties, however, I like to make larger than average down payments—sometimes as large as 50% because it lowers the risk and debt that needs to be serviced substantially and gives me a little breathing room in the event the project does not get turned around as quickly as I think. Just don't leave yourself too skinny on the project and risk running out of money because you are too highly leveraged.

The first thing you are going to want to do is find the 'go to' apartment lenders in your area. In earlier chapters I talked about how to do this so this should be easy. Follow those instructions and you will be just fine. Again, remember that we want lenders that specialize in this area and want to be competitive.

One quick but important note. Do not forget about Credit Unions. Credit Unions are great sources of financing IF they like commercial real estate and will be competitive. Some of the best financing packages we have put together have been from Credit Unions so don't just focus on banks. Okay?

So, assuming you have your list of banks/lenders here are the steps you need to follow in order to get your project financed.

1. Using the system outlined in this book, find the apartment property that is going to be a winner.

2. Once you have found that property make sure you put the property under contract of course 'subject to' being able to get adequate financing. Once you have the property under contract and have agreed to price and terms with the seller, you now create a business plan for the property that you want to finance. When you approach a lender make sure that you have a business plan for the property that spells out what you are trying to accomplish. I know when I say 'Business Plan' peoples eyes start to glaze over but I do have some good news that will help you on this that I will share with you in a moment. Remember, we are going to be raising the value of the property quickly and there will be some properties that, on the surface, may not look all that inviting before using our system on them and lenders get approached with blue sky deals on a daily basis. The business plan actually takes them through from start to finish what you are going to do to create massive amounts of value in a relatively short period of time. By using this method you will stand out and your project has a great chance in being financed.

Oh, the good news? If you go to www.9monthinvestment.com I have a sample business plan that you can download and use as a template for your next project and for any future projects.

3. Get the completed business plan to the lenders for their review. Make sure you are getting this in front of multiple lenders at once since they will vary on how competitive they will be at any

given time depending on how much money they want in loans. I suggest at least three if you can, and the more the better. Let me share a quick example with you as to why this is important.

I just closed on a 16 unit apartment property about a month ago. I had three financing proposals with interest rates from 5.5% - 6.35%. I had closing costs anywhere from $5,000 to zero. I had terms of anywhere from 3 years to 7 years. I figure I increased the cash flow about $944 per MONTH by having three proposals and going with the most competitive one. Make sure you do the same.

4. Choose the most competitive proposal and get the deal closed ASAP so you can start working on it and getting your value increased!

5. After you close on the project and as you are working on it, keep the lender updated with quick notes of your progress and let them know how it is going. By keeping the lenders informed it shows them you know what you are doing and they can keep lending you money time and time again.

6. Factor in 'lender time'. What I mean by this is lenders always want a ton of information from you on you and your project. This information gathering process and answering questions about the information on the project will take you longer than expected. Make sure you plan on this up front.

Not surprisingly, the key to an easy and profitable trip down financing lane is to have a great project in the first place. The better the project the easier this will be. The more a project is on the borderline the more convincing you will have to be. Again this is where your business plan will come in handy to assist you.

Step 11—Find good financing sources and stick with them. The key is to provide them your business plan and that format does all of the selling and heavy lifting for you. To download your free business plan, go to my site at www.9monthinvestment.com.

Chapter 13

The Secret To Being Able To Speed Up Your Progress In Reaching Your Real Estate Investment Success!

The purpose of this chapter is to really work with you to speed up your success, and through this process really 'tell it like it is'. There is a myth or two out there that is keeping people from achieving huge numbers in terms of financial growth through using our system, and I think it is important to take those on right now. I don't want any roadblocks, especially imaginary ones, to get in your way. So with that said I want to cover my top two things you really need to know, right now, in order for this system to work for you and make you a lot of money—no matter how much you want to invest in a property.

Truth is, when you are around this business long enough, even though the way WE make money is unique, you tend to hear or be exposed to some of the same things over and over again. The point of this chapter is to help you avoid the mistakes and to separate the good information from the bad.

#1 DON'T CONCENTRATE ON BEING A LOW OR NO MONEY DOWN INVESTOR.

Look, I am all about using as little of your cash as possible and maybe you are in the position that you do not have a lot of cash or money to invest. All that is fine and I will cover, in a later chapter, how to deal with this and get this system to work for you IF you do not have a nice chunk of money in your regular or IRA accounts yet. However, at this point it is important to understand this fact:

A) **Most of the no or low money down properties are the kind of properties you want to run away from and never buy and should be avoided for our system to work.**

Most properties that are low or no money down and the owner is willing to let them go with little or no down payment are terrible properties and will cost you more money, worry, aggravation, and frustration than you can imagine. Ask yourself this question: If a property is doing well and has a good track record, location, condition and tenant mix and is producing nice profits WHY does the owner have to sell it for no money or low money down? Truth is, if an owner has such a great property he does NOT have to sell it for no money down and in most cases would have a line of investors ready to buy it from him. Now, there IS that 1% of great properties where the owner may have fallen on hard financial times but keep in mind this is very rare. Most nice properties do not sell for now down payments and most are doing just fine.

So...

The reason most properties are offered for little or no money down is not because there is an owner financial problem, but because there is a property problem! If there is drug dealing going on in apartment 7, the tenants in apartment 12 are working on their motorcycle IN the apartment and they are selling guns out of apartment 5 do you really think this is the kind of property you want to own?? Even if you can get into it with low money down?

I know the last paragraph may have sounded a bit funny but it is from a real situation that I am aware of with a low money down purchase that a friend of mine was involved in. So the big reasons no or low money down deals will NOT work are:

1. Bad Location that will not improve in years.
2. Bad tenant mix and a property that will only attract bad tenants.
3. Weird converted home into sleeping rooms rented by the day or week.
4. Property structural problems that will cost tens of thousands to repair.

5. Property condition and location merit attracting tenants that will not pay rent on time, if ever, leading to massive vacancy and turnover costs.

So, make sure you understand that 99% of ALL properties being offered by owners with LOW or NO money down will fit into one of these five categories and make sure you also understand that IF they do you should avoid them.

Buying bad low or no money down properties can actually SLOW DOWN your progress.

B) Most People Buy A Low Money Down Property Simply Because They Can Buy A Low Money Down Property -- With Little Thought Into What They Are Exactly Buying.

Here is the problem. With all of the hype of low down investing what is the goal of low money down investors? Is it to find a great property? Is it to make a nice return? Is it to profit sooner vs. later? Actually, the answer to all of this is NO. Oddly enough, most low or no money down investors do NOT look to accomplish these things. Even though they set out to do this most of their attitudes change—whether they know it or not...

Huh? Well if that is not the case what are they doing then?

They are simply buying a property for low money down only because they can get it for low money down. Stop and read this sentence again please. The process shifts from buying a good property that will help me financially to finding a property to buy for low money down.

Think about this. The no or low money down investors attention shifts to finding a property for low or no money down. All they want to look at, analyze and inspect are no or low money down properties. Pretty soon they find themselves not in the profitable purchasing world but in the 'lets find that low or now money down property' world. They are no longer focused on profits because they start to assume that just because they can get into a property with low money down they will profit.

Do you see the difference?

Coupled with the fact that 99% of the low or no money down properties out there are properties that need to be avoided you now have potential problems on your hands because you are literally looking for a needle in a haystack aren't you? The odds are stacked against you already!

So what do most low down investors do? They buy a property for low money down that ends up costing them tens of thousands of dollars and hundreds of hours of work, time and frustration. This happens all the time.

THE SOLUTION TO THE LOW MONEY DOWN PROBLEM

So, what is the solution to all of this? What is the solution to avoiding making the same costly mistakes that so many others have made and will make with no or low money down investing??

Work your way from becoming a low money down investor into an investor that makes large down payments on properties. The simple system that I have outlined here should be able to assist you to that end.

You see the goal that you want to achieve here from using this system if not only making yourself wealthy faster and folding time, but it is also to go from a low or little money down investor to one that can make large down payments on properties and not have any issues with it.

Think about this:

1. Nice apartment properties usually sell for cash from financing.
2. Owners of nice apartment properties usually have no interest in selling for no money down simply because they don't have to.
3. With larger down payments you have more apartment properties to review and analyze that could be possible purchases for you, thus you can actually build your apartment empire faster.
4. The properties will cash flow better with less debt.
5. You have more equity in the properties from the very beginning giving you a huge advantage.

6. You have the power to 'move on' to the next deal if a certain property does not meet your criteria—with cash there is always another bus coming! With low down payment you have little to choose from.

So the majority of advantages goes to the person that has the cash to buy great deals as they come up, and that is really the main point of everything I have said—WHEN THEY COME UP!

Bottom line here is, you want to become the investor that is capable of buying apartments and investment property with large down payments as fast as possible because this puts you in a position of power and profit every time! There is nothing wrong with low or no money down real estate investing—but that is not a game you want to play permanently. You want to get out of that game as soon as you can for all of the reasons I mentioned in this chapter.

Many of the best projects I have owned, or my partners have owned have been a result of having cash to purchase them. The one with the money has the control. Make sure you work on getting yourself in that position as soon as possible.

Step 12–Make sure you avoid purchasing no or low money down property for the sake of purchasing. To make sure you make the right decision every time you can, download the No Money Down/Low Money Down questionnaire that you can fill out every time you are looking at a low or no money down property. www.9monthinvestment.com.

CHAPTER 14

THE SECRET IN THE WORLD OF REAL ESTATE THAT NO ONE WILL TELL YOU...

Over the last few pages I have gone over no or low down investing and why you want to be in that world for as little time as possible if you can help it. If you can't help it, then I suggest working your way to being able to pay large cash down payments for properties. So why go to the trouble of sharing this information with you??

Again, it is to speed up your progress. Conventional wisdom is NOT ALWAYS CORRECT!

I tell you this because there is a secret that most gurus will not share with you and it is something that has to be mentioned because again, knowing this WILL SPEED Up your progress.

THE SECRET is that the great deals come up when they are ready, not when you are ready. The great deals come in the size and shape they want not what you want. The great deals come in prices and values at what they want not what you want.

In other words your ideal project could be available tomorrow or six months from now...you never know which. **THE IMPORTANT THING IS TO ALWAYS BE READY TO TAKE ADVANTAGE OF A GREAT PROJECT WHEN THE OPPORTUNITY COMES UP...BECAUSE IT WILL.**

You see, you may have a goal and want to invest in a project that would be up to, say 36 units and you may want it to be in a certain area of the city and of a certain age only to find two months down of your search you find an excellent purchase that passes all our tests from earlier but it is an 18 unit property that is in another area of the city. Hmmm. Now what?

Point being...Do not limit yourself to certain property sizes and locations and do not limit your geography in your city. The caveats to these would be to make sure the locations ARE GOOD and to make sure you are not doing this in a market that you are NOT familiar with nor have the market information at your disposal that we talked about earlier.

You see, I have a lot of people partner with me to purchase investment real estate. Many of them are right now WAITING for me to find that great opportunity for them to get involved with me. Not surprisingly, some of them are getting impatient with me because I have not found the ideal project yet. I will of course find that project but my partners want it found NOW!!! THEY ARE READY NOW! Again, it does not work like that. We may go two more months before a great project appears and then more than likely another one will appear 4 days later—this up and down environment happens like this all the time.

So if you really want to avoid the wasted time and energy on items that will frustrate many—but won't frustrate you, read and commit this paragraph to memory.

You want to get into a position where you are and can make larger down payments because you always want to have enough power to purchase that great property whenever it may come up because you do not know when it will come up. The way to speed up your progress towards wealth is to be in a position to jump on a great project when the opportunity comes up. The BEST way to do that is to have as much cash and/or financing ready to go as you can. Despite what most guru's say, this IS the fastest way to a lot of wealth - fast. By using this in conjunction with the strategies of finding these projects in earlier chapters.

> **Step 13**–Make sure you understand that the fastest way to wealth is to invest in as many great projects as possible...WHEN THEY COME UP! The only way to do that is to become a cash generating buyer of projects as fast as possible!

Chapter 15

The Next Three Months—Adding Sources of Income And Reducing Your Expenses—Time To Enact The Rule of 9%

Ok lets catch our breath for a second. First we have gone through the process of knowing what kind of apartments to look for and what kind to avoid in order to explode our net worth (fold time) today not wait for decades.

Second, we know it is all about manipulating the numbers of the apartment properties and using the Rule of 9% in order to do this.

Third, we have learned how to negotiate a profitable price on the property and we have also found a source of financing for our purchase as well.

By this time you should have gone through all of these steps and finally closed on your first apartment property! Congratulations!

The first three months is really about working on all of the items previously discussed to make sure you not only stop any leaks that should not be going on in terms of 'cash flow leaks' but to also put your plan into place on getting the property up and running as smoothly and profitably from a cash flow standpoint.

Now is the time to really hit the rule of 9%. This is where you will make hundreds of thousands of dollars...if not millions. The good news is, as mentioned in the last chapter, we only have to cover two areas of the apartment investment in order to profit in a very short period of time.

1. Income coming into your hands from the property.

2. Expenses being paid by you to operate the property.

Assuming that you are on schedule the next 90 days means you need to start adding as much income to the property as you possibly can. The first three months was basically plugging any leaks in the property and taking care of any post closing issues but now we are at the most crucial time of the property ownership.

The good news is, this is actually pretty easy and you will have actually already started working on some of this by now but lets start really focusing on making our NET INCOME from the apartment property as high as possible right away.

What that said, here is what you need to be working on here in the next 90 days:

1. All rents to market levels or above.
2. All other income sources to market level or above.
3. All Possible Expenses reduced to their lowest possible number.

Let's cover each one of these briefly.

Rent at market levels or above: Of course, now is the time for rents to get to market level or maybe even pushed up more. I tend to push for a bit above market rate especially if the unit and complex are showing well at this point. I would be doing the same for units who have leases that are turning over. This is no time to be conservative—here you want to be aggressive since you are now establishing a baseline from where your rents will be in terms of future raises. In other words easier to raise it up to market level or more now vs. trying to do it over 6–12 months. Your property management folks you will have in place will have a good feel for this too, so your job is to concentrate on maximizing the rent—theirs is to deliver the news to the tenants.

Other income sources to market levels or above. Now is also the time to make sure that any other income streams that are coming into the property are maximized as well.

A great example here is coin operated laundry machines. Many investors and apartment owners do not give these machines much thought but in reality they can add hundreds of thousands of dollars to your bottom line.

For example. A couple of years ago I took over a 108 unit project. The property laundry machines were producing about $8,400 per year in income. About three months after taking over I doubled the cost of doing a wash and a dry. Result? This year we will have over $20,000 in income coming in FROM QUARTERS! Not only that, but that is almost $12,000 in additional income we will have coming in…AND ALL I DID WAS RAISE THE PRICE OF LAUNDRY. The best part? Our properties are now worth an additional $130,000 since I added $12,000 to the bottom line. Remember, all this took was raising the price of the laundry machines.

Now, the same goes for other vending machines as well like candy, soda, etc. Raise those prices. Always keep in mind that it is a HUGE INCONVENIENCE for a tenant to go somewhere else to save a $1.00, like a Laundromat. So, do not be afraid to not only maximize your rents but get all of the vending machines doing the same thing as well.

The other thing you may want to be considering at this point is, are there any other ways of the property producing more income? Can you squeeze even more money out of the tenants? Look outside of what is existing to see if you can come up with anything.

I will give you another example of this to get your juices flowing.

In most of our properties, we had high speed internet installed. At the tenants option they can pay an additional $35.00 per month, added to their rent, for the privilege of using the high speed internet connection. Our cost? $18.00 per month. So, on every unit that we have high speed internet in place, we are earning an additional $17.00 per month! You multiply that by about 100 units, we now have an additional $1,700 per month added to the bottom line! This is pure net income!

Do you see now how your property can become so much more valuable, faster??

On To Expenses:

Decrease your expenses now! Last chapter, I briefly discussed how to do this and what I thought I would do here is give you an easy to follow plan of getting your expenses reduced as soon as possible.

1. Focus on the largest expense and go down from there. The first thing you want to do is focus on getting the largest expenses reduced. For most people this would be property taxes. Remember, you probably would NOT have pursued this property if you thought there was no chance to reduce this expense so get on it. Many cities or counties drag their feet and have a long process of reducing a properties assessed value or the taxes paid. So get on this right away.

2. Once you are done with this then go to the next largest expense and so on. You get the picture?

Example: I just got done taking over an 8 unit property. The annual taxes are $12,000 per year—I know I can get them reduced to $7,200 creating almost $5,000 in additional cash flow and $50,000 in additional value. I have to start that process now in order for this to take effect the following year.

The process of reducing your expenses usually takes the least amount of time to execute but may take a longer time to see the results since in some cases it can be up to 6 months or more before those expenses are finally reduced. That is why you work on this right now.

Don't forget about other ways of reducing expenses. Another tip I have for you that will add tens of thousands of dollars to your bottom line is to start having the tenants pay for all of the utility costs even though their units may NOT be separately metered for such.

For example, in some of our properties there is one furnace that heats all of the units. So, as owners, we pay for the heat to those units. Not a good strategy, especially if you live in a climate that turns below zero temperatures in the winter time. So, what we did was for tenants that were on a month to month lease OR those tenants that had their leases turning over we left their rents the same BUT made them pay for their prorated share of heat for the building. In the property I am talking about, the monthly heating bill averaged $2,000 for 24 units. So, the tenants did not pay any additional rent but they did pay about $83.00 per month for heating costs. Just by doing this, it increased our cash flow substantially and our property value over $200,000! Again, all we did was have the tenant pay the heating bill!

Can you see how this can be so powerful in making your property worth more money?

The Best Strategy For This

The best strategy for raising income and reducing the expenses in this 90 day window is to do it all at the same time. If you can help it, do NOT work on just one expense at a time or one income item at a time until you have it completed—work on ALL of them at once or as many of them at once as you can! This will create fantastic momentum for you and you will have these items tackled well before the 90 days are up. Remember, you also have property management folks in place to really help you get this stuff done. If they are worth their salt, they will assist you with most or all of these processes but again, remember, you do NOT depend on them to do these things for you—you need to continually check and inspect to make sure these items are being taken cared of.

So, you have owned the property now for about 6 months. You have stopped the leaks and worked on your tenant mix and your occupancy. You have stopped the leaks in terms of your cash flow. You have also started to implement the rule of 9% and work on raising your income and reducing your expenses.

Now comes the fun part.

SECTION III—9 MONTHS LATER AND PROFITING FROM YOUR WORK

CHAPTER 16

SIX MONTHS LATER—POSITIONING THE PROPERTY TO SELL, REFINANCE OR HOLD.

At this point you are to be congratulated! If you have gotten this far 90% of the work is done. Your property should now be well on its way to making you tens to hundreds of thousands of dollars sometime in the next three months.

However, as I said our work is about 90% done, but I did not say 100% done. In order to assure yourself of that large profit you deserve, you now need to take the time to position the property to profit.

What do I mean by positioning the property?

Simple—Getting it ready to sell for the highest price possible or appraise for the highest price possible.

Let's talk about these in detail.

Getting the property ready to sell for the highest possible price.

Now is the time to make sure the property is at its best in terms of cash flow, high net operating income (due to implementing the rule of 9%) and condition.

How do you do this?

By understanding this very easy to remember secret on getting a ton of money for your apartment property—here it is.

THE LESS A BUYER WILL HAVE TO DO TO/FOR THE PROPERTY UPON TAKING OVER THE MORE MONEY THE BUYER WILL PAY FOR THE PROPERTY.

In other words the less time, hassle and energy that the buyer expects to expend on the property the more the property will sell for and the more that you will get.

For example, if the buyer has to kick out a bunch of tenants, do a bunch of repair and maintenance work to the property and deal with a bunch of rent collection issues you can expect Mr. Buyer wanting a heavy discount on the property.

But...

If the property is in good condition, if the tenant mix is good and responsible, if the rents are already at their highest level, if the expenses have already been reduced to their lowest number then my friend, you can expect to sell the property for pretty darn close to full price.

This should not come as surprise to you but many apartment property owners miss this and try to take a shortcut to profits. I want to save you months of time and thousands in profits...Here is what I mean.

Many people will buy an apartment property correctly. Using my system and locating the right apartment property they are on track.

But...

Right after they close they fall off the track because they do not want to do the necessary work to the income stream (raising income and reducing expenses) and the necessary work that the property may need. No, they want to just flip the property and put it on the market now and negotiate with a new buyer to take care of all of these items that are still on the list to be done.

My friend, if you do this and think "Oh the Hell with it—I will just negotiate this work in the deal and let the new buyer take care of it", you will more than likely fail.

Why?

One, because of what we just talked about. Whenever we have a lot of work in front of us we will pay less for a property. The new buyer will want to probably discount the crap out of the property.

Second, and more importantly. The new buyer does not know what we know and your attempts to educate him on this will only be seen as a tactic to get him to pay more money for the property. Believe me, I know from experience. Better to do the necessary work on the property FIRST and then sell it Okay?

So, now we want to act as if we would be buying this property over again in the next three months. We want everything to be in as close to perfect shape as we can get it because the more it looks like the new buyer can just walk in, take over and make money...the better.

So, specifically, what do we do?

1. Make sure all of your rents are at market levels or above.
2. Make sure your expenses have been reduced as much as possible.
3. Make sure your other sources of income are now at their maximum levels.
4. Make sure you have implemented any other sources of additional income coming into the property at it maximum capacity.
5. Make sure if you are passing through expenses to tenants, such as water, gas, etc. that you have this in place by this time.
6. Inspect ALL UNITS, GROUNDS, ETC. If you cannot be at the property make sure you have your property management folks do this. You want to make sure there are no surprises waiting for the new buyer that may make him want to discount the property (like a leaking roof in one of the top floor units you were not aware of). Also, this goes a long way to see if you still have any tenant problems that the buyer may not be happy about.

Again, nothing more than making sure the project is running at full capacity. If it is not taking the necessary time with your property management folks to see that it is running where it needs to be. The only difference is, now you should have deadlines in place for everything to be ready for a new buyer. Make sure your property management folks are aware of those deadlines.

Getting the Property To Appraise For the Highest Price Possible.

You may be already asking yourself what this means. Isn't this the same thing that we just covered in selling for the highest price possible?

Actually no.

You see, the goal here is not selling but refinancing and pulling as much cash out of the property to do this again! That is the goal here and in order for us to reach that goal—to be able to not only keep a property that is now operating at maximum capacity and producing large cash flows and adding hundreds of thousands of dollars to our bottom line AND doing it again with another property.

For example. Not that long ago I purchased an apartment property for $2,650,000. I proceeded to take it through the 9 Month Investment System and once I was done the property was worth $4,200,000. A profit of $1,600,000! All within a one year time period!!

Anyway, I did not want to sell the property, I wanted to keep it because in my mind this was a great long term investment. Don't get me wrong, great short term but also a great long term deal as well. So, I decided to keep it.

I then contacted a lender and asked to refinance the property. I wanted to pull out down payment money to do this same thing on another property that I had located. So, knowing that I took about 60 days to get the property ready for an appraisal—an appraisal at its highest value I might add.

What happened?

The property appraised at $4,400,000. I got to borrow 80% of that amount or $3,520,000. I owed about $1,800,000 on the property so I got to pull out $1,700,000 to purchase my next property! That's what I call NONE OF MY OWN MONEY DOWN! Do you see how powerful this strategy can be?? Not only can you make a ton of cash you can also make a ton of money, reinvest and do it again!

So how do you get a property ready to appraise for its highest possible price and accomplish these kinds of wealth building moments? Simple, follow the instructions that I gave in getting the property to sell for as much money as possible. Same thing only instead of selling you are looking at refinancing the property instead. Once you have gone through the checklist and accomplished everything then get in touch with the lender and have the meeting, letting them know you want to refinance the property and do what you just got done doing to this property…to another!

***One important note about this. The lender, NOT YOU, decides who will appraise the property. Make sure the lender has an experienced apartment property appraiser doing this! More than likely you will not have to worry about this since lenders that operate in this league typically do know what they are doing. However, when the appraiser does inspect the property and does a walk through, make sure that you accompany them so they not only have an accurate idea as to the important items of the physical property but also have YOUR NEW ACCURATE NUMBERS in order to perform the appraisal—not the old numbers!

One final note on this chapter. The last thing that I mentioned is not do anything. You can of course go through this entire process and bank the EQUITY you have built up as well and not sell nor refinance.

So, using my example above, I could have just held onto the property and kept my loan of $1,800,000 in place with the value being $4,400,000. The equity here, $2,600,000 would be mine to tap into when I wanted. Also, I would be adding an additional $2,600,000 to my net worth—again in a matter of months! Of course, at the same time I would be profiting from the property through its monthly cash flows as well all while the value would keep increasing and my debt would keep going down.

So how do you make the decision of which way to go? Sell, Refinance or just Keep It?

Well of course, part of this decision will be based on whether you are involved in a private partnership and there may be language that specifies what you have to do in this situation. If you are using Private Money then the same thing may be true here as well. So, sometimes the course of action will already be spelled out for you even before you get to this point.

But if you are not tied down to a decision at this time, what do you do?

Simple. You proceed with what you think is the most profitable action at the time. Once you have the property in position then you take a look at your goals and decide which way is the best way to proceed, based on where you are in your financial world. Simple as that.

> **Step 14**–It is smart to position the property to sell at this point even if you decide not to. Once this is done decide if you want to sell, refinance or hold the property. In any case you will have made your money in either cash or equity. Choose what is in your best interest at the time in terms of what it will take to accomplish your goals. For more tools from choosing a broker to sell your property to analyzing your costs of sale go to www.9monthinvestments.com.

CHAPTER 17

FINDING THE WARREN BUFFET OF REAL ESTATE

We are coming to the conclusion of this book. You have had the curtain peeled back and found out how to really profit in a very, very large way from apartment property investments using my 9 month system, AND while doing so putting as much work and effort into it as you would your typical stock portfolio, except the wealth gains are more massive using my methods.

It is at this time when the path has been laid out in front of many people on how to do this and get started on their properties, that I usually get the question from a number of people who lead very busy lives and are swamped busy with either job, career, family or all of the above and then some. I get the question:

"Hey Darin, I want to take this on, and want to get into at least a couple of apartment projects, as you have described, within the next 12 months and really explode my net worth—The 9 month system is great thing not only for my 'regular' monies but for my IRA money as well. However, I am swamped with work, family, responsibilities, volunteering, etc. Is there a way where I can basically have all this done for me???? Is there a resource out there that can take the ball from me so to speak and get it over the goal line???

Let me answer that question this way:

Now that we know that we need to invest in an apartment property that meets our 9 month investment criteria and you have absolutely NO TIME for this, you now need to simply call or find Warren Buffet.

What? What did I say? Yep, we need to find Warren Buffet. Go ahead, take some time to do this right now.

No problem, he is in Omaha isn't he? Okay, just pick up the phone and call him.

Okay, okay, by 'finding' him that is not what I mean exactly. You don't really have to find him, but what you do have to do is follow along with me here because it is very important.

You see, if you do any reading or studying of Mr. Buffet, you find out that bottom line is, he is very good at valuing businesses. Both publicly traded and not. He became very good at analyzing a business and seeing its relative worth vs. what the market thought it was worth. If he saw value there or thought he could buy the company at a discount, then he loaded up on the companies stock. He also did this with other businesses as well. Bottom line is, Buffet can look at a publicly traded or private business and tell you if it is a good deal at the current asking price for the stock or tell you what would be a good deal. In a nutshell, this is how Buffet and his investment partners grew rich…by his ability to spot and buy a good deal and do it over and over again. Period.

So, the question then becomes how? How did Buffet do this? Or, how DOES Buffet do this? How does he know so much vs. every other investor out there? Feel free to go and read his biography—it is pretty good and there are some other books on Buffet as well. I have read some of them but not all. When it comes to Buffet's success, you really don't need to read all of his books or even go to Omaha to figure out how he did it. These books will give you good personal insights behind the scenes of Buffets life, and the deals gone well and some gone bad.

But bottom line is he is very good at this investment in companies stuff. He is the best. Not many can even come close.

Well, how did he do it?? How did he become THE BEST? Here comes the simple answer about a simple man….

He has basically spent almost every waking moment of his life analyzing companies. From the time he was a kid, through high school and college at Columbia University almost every waking moment was spent working on this skill. Working on analyzing, buying and if necessary expanding or selling off companies. Every moment spent on good acquisitions and even bad ones. Yes, Buffet has had some bad ones too. But, in reality Buffet has become so good because his life's work, even at the expense of his relationships with his wife and others close to him at times, has been spending huge chunks of time analyzing and profiting from purchasing companies and businesses.

Buffet has gotten his skill at being a successful investor because it has been his life's work—to continually work and hone this skill.

Not only has this hard work on this skill made Buffet extraordinarily wealthy, it has made many others that partnered with him wealthy as well. It is not widely known but there are quite a few people that originally partnered with Buffet when he just got started—pooling their money together so he could use it to buy good deals.

Of course, those people are very wealthy today as well.

But here is my question, and believe me I am coming full circle here. Why did these people partner with Buffet? Why did they seek him out?

Here are the 4 MAIN reasons:

1. They knew from all the work and study he had done in the past that he was an expert, trusted his decision making and his background as well as what he was going to do in the future - which was work on their investments.

2. They did not have enough time themselves to be the same kind of expert as Buffet. No way could they replicate what he did and does on a daily basis to be this good at this. Easy decision for them to not spend their life on this—let Buffet do it.

3. They knew he was a REAL partner that had spent and will spend his career on taking a look inside and outside of these companies and businesses. He did not just sit behind a desk and tell some subordinate to do this stuff. Buffet himself does a lot of investigative work on these companies and businesses before making any investment decisions and still does.

4. He has his own money in the game. He was not playing just with other people's money. He has his own money in these investments and he treats them that way.

If you want to sum it up in one sentence, people partnered with Buffet because he is one of the few that had put in enough time, effort, and energy to be really, really good at valuing businesses and profiting from those businesses. Just like a professional athlete who puts in countless hours behind the scenes to be very good at what they do (think Tiger Woods) so did Buffet and that is why people will 'bet on Buffet'.

IN ESSENCE, THE REAL REASON PEOPLE PARTNERED WITH BUFFET IS THEY BOUGHT SPEED. THERE IS NO WAY THESE PEOPLE COULD INVEST THE TIME NECESSARY TO BE AS GOOD AS BUFFET SO IN ORDER TO BUY SPEED (FOLD TIME) THEY PARTNERED WITH BUFFET TO GET THOSE PROFESSIONAL INVESTOR RESULTS WITHOUT PUTTING IN THE NECESSARY LEARNING AND EXPERIENCE. THEY USED BUFFET AS THEIR LEVERAGE TO BE EXPERT STOCK MARKET INVESTORS.

So, why all of this talk about Buffet anyway? What's the point especially when we just got done talking about the subject of TIME at the beginning of the book and how precious it is and how difficult it is to find any more of it? Am I suggesting that now you need to be like Buffet and spend the time doing this too?

No, the good news is that I don't expect this at all so you can relax on that part, however, in order to make as much money from your apartment properties as fast as possible, you need to be just like the people that 'found' Warren Buffet. Find a person that has the same traits in the real estate world as Buffet and partner with them and use their expertise as your time leverage!

Let me illustrate by using me as an example.

The main reason that people partner with me to invest in Heartland of America real apartment properties is because I provide them speed. Yes, it is true that my partners want someone that is professional, has a good track record, and has the ability to spot a fantastic apartment project for them to own, one that will really grow their wealth at sometimes unbelievable speeds. But I provide them a huge amount of leverage, and they profit from my knowledge, experience and my years of work. In a sense, they become me when they partner with me and they do not have to learn a lick about any real estate related issues or matters—only if they want to.

This is what you need to do:

You need to find the Warren Buffet of real estate in your market or where you would like to invest because this is the faster ticket to the fast wealth building we have been talking about. By aligning yourself with a Warren Buffet of real estate it speeds up the process immensely AND you avoid mistakes along the way not to mention again it saves you a lot of personal time. Again, you are buying speed. To do it any other way may cost you way too much time and energy.

So you need to find someone who is very good in the world of commercial real estate and become one of their partners. A Warren Buffet of real estate if you will. Now, don't panic there will be a lot of things I will go over with you so you can avoid bad partner experiences. I will go over all of the questions you need to ask to screen the good ones from the bad or even the mediocre, so just bear with me. Remember, we are in search of SPEED here and I know you do not have 10–15 years to spend on becoming a market expert. I will now give you the litmus test you should use in order to become aligned with a 'Warren Buffet' of real estate.

1. They need to have at least 10 years experience in apartment property brokerage.

2. They need to have at least 7 years experience as an apartment property owner

3. They need to provide you with at least three references (names and phone numbers) of people who have done business with them and would do business with them again.

4. They need to provide you at least one example of how they made their clients or investment partners money on a real estate transaction.

Much like everything else, book reading and University degrees can only get you so far. In real estate, especially apartment properties, it takes a lot of experience to become really good at what you do. Real estate markets and cycles do not last a few months here and there, so you want to have someone that has had the experience of both a good market and a bad market as well as someone who has had experience selling apartment properties as well as owning them.

Bottom line is, when you get hooked up with someone that has this kind of experience, they will be able to spot opportunities much faster as well as help you avoid mistakes that could cost you tens of thousands of dollars.

The other part of this, that is actually good news, is that this will thin the herd of potential candidates substantially. Leaving you with just a few folks that you can contact and see if they would have an interest in assisting you in finding these kinds of apartment projects.

So, where do you start your search? You start by contacting your attorney and letting him or her know you want to start working with someone that is very good at finding good apartment deals and see who they may be able to recommend. Also, asking around through word of mouth is also a good idea. Lastly, if you still do not have anyone on the line yet, you may want to contact commercial real estate brokerage companies and ask for the apartment specialist on staff. There should be someone in the office that mainly does apartments. This is the person you want to talk to.

Again, big caution here. Make sure you have them follow the four items above. There are some folks that are all talk and have nothing to show for it AND are looking to possibly make a fat commission. Make sure you take them through this litmus test again with these easy to ask four questions.

On my website I have a questionnaire that you can send or email these guys when looking for someone that will work for you. It's a simple Q and A item that when answered gives you some good things to use and go on.

Also, remember, if these guys ARE GOOD then they are not waiting to take your call or email, so if you do not get immediate response do NOT let that bother you—they are probably working with other established clients but they should be back to you in a matter of 24–48 hours. Also, I prefer phone messages vs. email since emails can get lost that much easier.

Lastly, if you run into a roadblock here and you still feel you want it ALL DONE FOR YOU simply call my office and we can schedule a time to chat. Many of my partners from all over the US have done very well by working with me on Heartland of America property that is OUTSIDE of their marketplace. We have, for the most part, been very, very profitable. My system is already in place and I can welcome you if you want. You can let me know by going to my website and clicking on "So You Want To Work With Darin Garman"

> **Step 15**–A great way to leverage yourself is to find the 'Warren Buffet of real estate' in your market or become a Member of My Elite Investment Group. www.9monthinvestment.com.

CHAPTER 18

HAVING ALL OF THIS DONE FOR YOU.

This will not be a big chapter but I felt that I owed it to you, the reader, to make your 9-month journey towards your seven figures investment EVEN SHORTER AND EASIER.

Even shorter?? Easier??

Yep. As you have seen in this book, even though the 9-month system involved apartment properties that can sometimes be a bit overwhelming, my system is pretty easy to understand. You do not necessarily have to have a real estate background nor do you need to know a lot about property management, fixing things, being a landlord, etc. Simply put, you need to know what the market is doing now and where it is realistically going and how the opportunity you are looking at fits into that. As long as you can do this and "know your numbers" you are about 98% of the way there.

However, even if you do this it does require you to work and does require some of your time and simply put does require some risk. Yes I did say risk—even though in my mind this is the lowest risk kind of real estate ownership and investing there is some risk to it no two ways around it.

When I bring up the "R" work and the "T" word (Risk and Time) many people do start to become a bit agitated because of these two things. They get agitated because these are the two things that, more often than not, get in the way of getting going on this faster and with more enthusiasm. In other words, it all sounds good in the book but when it comes to you ACTUALLY taking action the R and T word always start to come up don't they?

The way to mitigate that risk and even spend little if any time on this is to simply have the 9-month system done for you. How? By partnering with an expert that will do all of the heavy lifting in terms of finding the property, qualifying it, financing it, getting the legal work done, closing it, working on it to build the profits and then ultimately selling the property—all you do is invest in it—your expert does the rest!

Again, you can have someone do all this for you, with your investment while you are busy doing other things. Also, when you get someone experienced that can really take a lot of the risk element out, don't you agree?

You see, this is why a majority of the people contact me. They want the results as if they spent the time and the energy in their market doing all of the things you need to do, but frankly do not want to take the risk, spend the time or CAN'T spend the time on this. So, they call me, the expert, to do it for them and give them these results without them changing anything in their daily routines.

So, how does it typically work? What should you expect in a similar kind of arrangement? Well let me give you an idea as to how I operate.

Let's say you contact me and tell me you want to be one of my Private Clients that has this process literally done for them. You want "IN" on my next 9 month investment. Great!

After we talk, I get some questions answered from you, and then proceed to find a property that is going to require $100,000 in down payment to purchase assuming of course that $100,000 was the amount of money you wanted to invest in a great project. I am now turned loose to find that project that you can get involved in.

Okay, fast forward. Let's assume that enough time has gone by and I now I have the property that passes all of our litmus tests and is one that will profit in a huge, huge way. What's next?

I simply contact you to see if you are interested in investing all or part of the $100,000 into a partnership that I would put together between you and me, and maybe a few others. You take a look at the property and decide if it is right for you and is as good as I say that it is. All of the details are shared with you; we take the time to go through all of your questions, concerns, etc. If you decide that after all of this information from me that it is as good as I say it is, we form a partnership and invest in the property and take it through the 9-month system with me in charge of making the process work the best I can. Of course if you decide that this is NOT the deal for you it is a matter of simply letting me know and we move on to the next possibility. Simple as that...

Again, all the heavy lifting done for you.

So the question is why? Why would I do this for you? Another question that needs to be answered is why should you consider this yourself?

As for why I (or someone like me) would do this, it is because it provides opportunities for everyone involved where none existed previously. It provides the ability to use skills and talents needed and used to identify great apartment projects to be used as much as possible. In other words, my bank account is not infinite. I honestly do not have enough money in my own bank account to take advantage of all great real estate projects as they come up. Being the "Go To Guy" allows me to take advantage of all projects that make sense if I choose to but there are always some that will come up that I cannot take advantage of because I had capital tied up in other properties.

It used to be that I would locate two or three projects at one time and was only able to take advantage of owning one of them and the other two would get away. That was tough.

Now being the "Go To Guy" for real estate investors allows me to take advantage of every GOOD project as long as it passes our tests rather than losing out on one because there would not be enough capital.

So, not only do I get to be involved in more projects, I also get to profit from more projects. I want to own as many profitable projects as I can.

As for why someone such as yourself would consider being teamed up with someone that did do this Heavy Lifting, has really already been covered in terms of taking the Risk and the Time element out it as much as possible. The other thing that is nice is that, it provides for all parties to not only diversity and to LOWER their individual risk, it also allows all parties to leverage their investment more by getting involved in higher value properties. You can now invest in a $5,000,000 property using this system where before you may have been able to pull off a $400,000 investment property at the very most.

Of course we have already discussed the obvious reasons in terms of not having to spend any time looking at property or analyzing it. Even though after reading this book you will KNOW how to do that it does not necessarily mean that you WANT or HAVE TIME to do it. Knowing what kind of project you want to use to explode your wealth is enough—now send someone else out there to do all the dirty work.

Another is that you do not need to be concerned that someone is going to SELL you something vs. bring you IN on an investment property. There is a key difference. When you team up with a "Go To Guy" that has their own money in the project as well the self interest part of this changes. For example, I have no interest in owning a property that is going to be a pain in the butt. None! I ONLY want properties that are going to perform day in and day out and be great deals and build wealth fast. So, if you partner with me on a project you know you are getting the real thing that is going to get you to your financial goals faster vs. being sold a property that MIGHT get you there IF you are lucky.

Knowing your "Go To Guy" has skin in the game is a big deal and goes a long way to help you decide who to work with. If your "Go To Guy" does not have skin in the game that should be a red flag. Not a deal killer but a red flag.

Then there is the management and logistical side of this. Your "Go to Guy" should provide you with the finding of the property, the financing of it, purchase of it and closing of it. All under one umbrella. Also, they should do all of the things necessary to get that property to maximum profit and cash flow as soon as possible. In other words, they would be the point person from finding it and purchasing it to managing it to selling it. All done for you.

Then there is the mistake part of this which I guess is part of the risk. Of course after going through this information thoroughly you can have all of your I's dotted and T's crossed and still make a mistake. This is a way to avoid mistakes and not having to worry about the project or stay awake at night. So, you can avoid making a Rookie Mistake if you want.

Profitable Strategies Combined?

What quite a few of my clients and partners do is both. They will look for apartment property opportunities in their own 'back yard' while working with me at the same time and getting involved in the opportunities that I happen to locate. Covering both of these bases gives them more projects to look at, consider and invest in.

Obviously the more projects you have to look at, the more you get to cross your desk on a local and a national level the faster your wealth can increase. However, the first thing you should really do after reading this book is decide what 'camp' you are going to be in 1) Do it yourself. 2) Have your "Go To Guy" do it. 3) Both. After you make that decision commit to it and get moving.

Lastly, it really gets back to leverage. Not so much leverage in terms of borrowing money but when you can pool your resources with others that are working toward the same goal it gets you into bigger and in most cases better properties too because you are using the leverage of other people—Your "Go To Guys".

Always remember that the more and larger the properties that you control the larger your jumps in net worth will be—the larger your cash flows will be and the faster you will attain your wealth goals. Having someone do it for you may be just the piece of this puzzle that gets you to where you want to be with more speed and less stress.

So, for all parties involved it provides pooling of everyone's resources to use smart leverage to profit more with LESS risk to the individual investor and this is where your "Go To Guy" comes into play. Directing you towards the best situations where you can safely leverage your investment in ways that may make other jealous.

Step 16–Now is the time to decide whether or not you want to do this yourself, or have your "Go To Guy" do it or do both. There is a questionnaire to help you answer this and come to a conclusion of what should work best for you. You can complete this questionnaire by going to www.9monthinvestment.com.

FINAL CHAPTER

Over the course of this book we have everything that I said we would in the first chapter. We have folded time. In the big picture we have taken an investment amount and changed the game. What would take you 5–10–15 years to achieve in terms of your wealth can now be done in 9 months. My clients, partners and I have proven this on more than one occasion.

So what will you do? You have the means to literally fold time now in terms of your return and growth of wealth and investment. The good news is you can really go one of two ways. The first is of course you doing it yourself. You have the necessary tools, steps and strategies to take it to the next level and become the Warren Buffet of real estate within your market. You can have some nice real estate holdings producing large profits for you and you don't have to be a professional real estate investor to do it.

If that is not your gig and you have no interest in doing this yourself you can find someone to do it for you. Find a Darin Garman in your market to do all of the legwork for you while you spend time on other things. If this person follows the rules that you have outlined it makes sense to even split the profits with him or her. Smart move. If nothing else you can team up and partner with me on my next project and have the benefits of being my partner and working with me exclusively. If you have an interest in being my partner on my next project simply go to my website at www.9monthinvestment.com and sign up. There is a non-refundable deposit that you need to place to be one of my partners so it is only for the serious but again—it will save you a lot of time and get you the results that you are looking for.

Lastly, you have the tools here to become a very wealthy person OR grow what wealth you have in massive chunks vs. the conventional plodding along. Again, this is NOT get rich quick but it is get wealthier faster than conventional methods. I am all for that. Again, real estate is just a means to an end—that is making you wealthier than you are today and doing it much faster. Take advantage of this information and use it and please keep me posted and let me know how you are doing.

If anything else at least get hooked up with us and keep hooked up with us by getting on our email list. Again www.9monthinvestment.com.

Good luck and please keep me posted with your success stories.

All the best.

Darin Garman
America's Apartment and Investment Property Specialist
743 10th St.
Marion, IA 52302
FAX 1-866-212-2838
Email: Darin_Garman@msn.com

BONUS CHAPTERS TO HELP YOU PUT EVEN MORE MONEY IN YOUR POCKETS FROM APARTMENTS—EASIER!

Bonus Chapter 1

Fast And Easy Methods Of Choosing Your Property Management Company, Attorney, And Accountant To Do All The Work For You.

Your job again is to use great untapped apartment properties to make as much money as possible in the shortest period of time. Your job is not to take weeks and even months trying to find a winner in the world of property management, accounting, and law. Look, I am not trying to talk you out of being careful here but many GURUS would spend entire SEPARATE chapters on just who you should use as an attorney, accountant, and property manager and how to go about interviewing and selecting them.

Let me give you my shortcut steps to have an attorney, accountant, and property manager in place in less than a week AND I will only take a short chapter on how to do this FOR ALL THREE! Sound good? Okay, let's go.

The first thing to do:

Start this process now. Do not wait until you have a property under contract. You want to be working on this before you find a property. Get these folks in place and ready to work with you now! Especially the attorney who may be assisting you with your purchase or looking over any documentation.

Choosing An Attorney.

I will number the simple to follow instructions here for you to use to shortcut finding a great real estate attorney.

1. Ask your commercial brokers. Commercial brokers know who the 'go to' real estate attorneys are in the market. Ask two or three brokers to give you two or three names each of the top attorneys in your market that do mostly commercial real estate properties.
2. Ask the lenders. Call the same lenders you talked to in the earlier chapters and ask them who the best real estate attorneys are in the market. Again, have them give you two or three each if they can.
3. Ask other apartment owners. While you are doing your mailings and other work to land some apartments as part of the conversation ask these guys who their attorney is and who they use.
4. Call your title company and speak to the manager. Ask the manager which attorney in town is known to do the most work in the world of commercial real estate.

That's it! After you go through this process you will have two or three names that will be repeated. Those are the guys you target to represent you.

This process should not take you more than 2 hours.

Your next step is to call them and schedule a meeting with them. Let them know you plan on purchasing some apartment units in the near future and you heard they were the person to work with and you wondered if you could come in and chat with them for around 15 minutes, about what you are looking for and what you want to accomplish. They will oblige.

Once you are in their office, let them know what you are up to and what you plan on doing and that you would like their assistance. Try to get a feel for how well you would work together. The attorney that you think provides you the best fit and can give you the necessary time to work on your projects is the one to go with. Also, you want to gauge how busy this person is. You do want to work with a person that is busy and has business coming in at a steady clip—that tells you that they are successful. One thing you want to see though is how busy they are. You want someone that can work with you and respond to you as well as get some legal work done for you in a reasonable period of time.

A side note. It is very helpful if you have an attorney working with you that is also an owner in investment real estate. If one of your finalists is also a real estate owner too this is a plus and you should consider this a sign to work with them.

Once you have talked with two or three attorneys decide on one to work with and get started with them.

Property Manager

In terms of finding a great property management company you will want to go through the same process as for the attorney. You will want to ask your commercial brokers for their recommendations. You will also want to ask the lenders too. You will want to speak with other apartment owners as well. Place most of your weight in the comments from what you hear out of your brokers and apartment owners. They will know best here. In this process you can skip talking to the title company.

(If you need a refresher on this please see the previous chapters where I outline this when talking to lenders and commercial real estate brokers.)

Again, after a few of these conversations there will be two or three that come up. Sit down with the manager of the company and talk with them about your goals and plans and see if you can get a feel for how they can help you.

Two important things to ask the manager of the property management company while meeting with them:

1. How many units do they currently manage and are they able to add more without much of a problem?

2. Do they own apartment units themselves?

If a management company is managing thousands of units and it looks as if they are running at full capacity and about to burst with no intention of adding any staff then you may want to avoid this company. They may take you on and not do the job they should do because you are customer #455. You want a management company that has experience and room for your future purchase as well.

Also, you want to avoid management companies that own their own apartment units if you can. This is too big of a conflict of interest. I mean you have a vacancy that needs filled and so do they...which one do you think gets filled first? Of course—theirs does. There is nothing wrong with management companies owning their own units just make sure that you do not use a company that does. Now, if they own a few here and a few there I could probably live with it but if they own say 150+ units then that spells trouble in my mind. I have seen investors units sit empty while the project across the street owned by the management company is fully occupied.

Lastly a good attorney knows good property management companies. If you settle on an attorney they would be the person to ask on this issue as well.

Finding An Accountant.

Again, your attorney will be a good person to ask on this as well as your commercial real estate brokers. You want to make sure that you use an accountant that has a lot of experience with real estate properties and partnerships -- not one that mainly works on 1040's. Accountants that know what they are doing have saved me literally tens of thousands of dollars in taxes!

As an option after speaking with the attorney and commercial real estate broker, you can ask your property manager as well.

Bonus: Having an accountant that actually owns commercial investment real estate as well. The owners of the accounting firm that I use also own apartment properties as well and are familiar with using the most advantageous ways for me and my partners to profit and pay less in taxes.

Caution: Always keep in mind that when you work with the best you will pay for it. Expect the fees for all of the folks to be a bit higher than what MOST typically charge. Long story short, more than likely it is worth the added expense in the long run, so pay the money. My experience has been that the money, aggravation and frustration these folks will save you will be more than worth their cost.

Another way of looking at the process that I have outlined for you here is that what this does for you is that it helps you avoid having to hire any employees during this process, or having any staff around that you have to manage. As you can see, this is all basically outsourced in one way or another with you not having to be concerned about anyone working for you.

Lastly, I want you to make sure you basically go through people with experience to find your attorney, accountant, and your property manager vs. just opening the yellow pages or doing a Google search and then just picking someone that sounds good. This is far too important to leave to chance. Talk with the folks that have experience in the real estate business first.

> **Bonus Step**–Assemble the rest of your power team. Use the suggestions here in the chapter to not only shortcut your search but to get the best people on board with you than you can find. For a punch list of directions to follow to get the best property manager, accountant, and attorney simply log on to www.9monthinvestment.com.

BONUS CHAPTER 2

HOW TO SELL PARTNERS AND/OR PRIVATE LENDERS ON YOUR DEAL.

No matter what, if you are looking for someone to partner with you on the next project you find, or if you are looking for Private Money, there a few nuances to actually *selling the deal* to those that show interest that can be really valuable. I am going to share a few tips and strategies that will shortcut your start with this, and then have you not only act like a real estate PRO but also have you getting the results of a pro!

The bottom line here is, you want people to be involved in your project with the least amount of hassle and resistance. Follow these tips to get that to happen.

Here are the 5 Golden Rings to Selling Someone On Your Next Project.

1. <u>Remember—Take away selling</u>. Elsewhere in this book, I talk about the importance of takeaway selling but I will hit the high point here. Make sure you come across like it is THEM who are missing out if they do not take advantage of it, not you! Your posture is never to be one in need! Never forget that. Again, I devote an entire section in this book to this.

2. <u>Do NOT think your prospects are sophisticated investors and show them a ton of charts, graphs and other information that would take a physicist years to figure out</u>. This is the exact OPPOSITE of what they want and expect. Look, 99.9% of the investors want simple information and do not want the information you provide them to give them a headache! You

want to make sure you give them enough information so they can make an informed decision as to whether they should move ahead on the deal or not. The easiest way is to have a one or two page description of the property you are proposing followed by income and expense information. The income and expense information should show how much money the property is making right now, and should have a second sheet on how much, realistically, the property should make once you are done taking it through our 9 month system. The information should also have a few color photos of the property as well. I have an example of what your information should look like posted at www.9monthinvestment.com.

3. Have more than one way to make money from the property. This is probably the most important ring of the 5 rings. The key to get maximum participation from your fellow investors, whether or not they are going to be private lenders or partners of yours, is to have more than one way to make money.

For example, if you are going to invest in a 36 unit property and the purchase price is $800,000 I would be showing the investors how they will make money from: 1. Cash flow. I will show them how well the property will be cash flowing either in the near term, or once we are done taking it through our system 2. Appreciation. On top of the cash flow, I will show my investors how much the property will go up in value as well. 3. Annual Return just on cash flow. I would show them what the annual return on the investment would be just from the cash flow. 4. Overall return with cash flow, appreciation, equity build up, etc. I would also show them what the return would be on the property overall, cumulative including if and when we sell the property.

Now, compare this method to that of one where I just show them how much cash flow the property will be producing, and do not talk about any other ways the property will make us money. I could still be a little convincing using this method, but not as convincing as if I had not one, but four ways that they would be making money. Always show more than one way the property will make money!

4. <u>If Things Do Not Go As Planned We Still Make Money Method</u>. This is a very important part of selling your project to a private investor or a partner—it is talking about the fact that even if it does not work out as we say, we will STILL make money. Most people would shy away from using this because they would be afraid it would punch holes in the project, or bring up objections on the project from possible investors BUT it does not work that way. You see most people are used to getting the IF IT ALL WORKS OUT LIKE WE THINK IT WILL pitch. You know what I mean—it happens in everything—from real estate to network marketing. You know, "All you have to do Darin is get three people under you and then they get three people under them and so on, after 1 year IF IT ALL WORKS OUT, you will have 76 people under you producing huge sums of money for you." Well, people are like this in their approach to get you into *something* all the time. You want to be different. You want to show them the scenario of even IF it does not work out like we think—and a kind of worse case scenario happens we still make money and here is how we do it.… That is your approach. I guarantee that if you use this it will work—of course your project needs to be good enough to work out if your projections are off—but you need to explain this to them as well in your conversation and your pitch.

5. <u>Lastly, have something about the project that you do not like and bring it up.</u> Yes, you want to bring up something about the property that does not excite you or it could even bother you. For example, I was on the phone yesterday to a group of investors and we were discussing how we would be possibly purchasing a 24-unit project. Right away in our phone conversation, I talked about what I liked about the property and then I started to talk about what I did NOT like about it. In this case, it was the older appliances and the older counter tops and floor coverings in the property. I went on to tell them that if I had my way I would get rid of these appliances and counter tops and that we may have some capital expense in doing that in the near term and that it may not produce much in the way of cash flow for the next few months.

By now, you are probably asking yourself why in the world would I do that—especially if no one brings it up? Again, there is no perfect property and 99% of people know this—if you have a project that has NO problems associated with it that does MORE for bringing up skepticism than by always talking on just the good parts—always remember that. You must, I repeat you MUST talk about the parts of the property that are not that attractive. By doing this you will show that you not only have a project that they can believe in but that you are a straight shooter. Even though this may sound counterintuitive, this ALL bodes well for you.

Before I leave the subject of damaging admission, let me share something with you. You need to make sure that the property has more good than bad and that it is genuinely a good project and that even the things that are NOT RIGHT are minor in comparison to what kinds of profits you will be making. I know this may sound a little like common sense, but I can put up with some old appliances and countertops vs. having a serious environmental problem and rocket fuel dripping into my apartment. So, make sure that you have a project that is THAT GOOD and that despite its shortcomings that it will still be a good deal.

You can also present your project in this manner as well to an institutional lender, but I would use caution with this. Many banks and institutional lenders will take old appliances as meaning the entire project needs a rehab—they tend to over exaggerate to protect themselves. If you do decide to use the 5 rings with a bank or similar lender, be very conservative with your choice of words and what you disclose to them. Show them the various ways this will make money. Not one way.

Again, use these 5 rings on every project that you present to a potential partner or private equity lender and chances are you will be able to get your financing—no matter where your financing is coming from.

Bonus Step–Make sure you use the 5 gold rings of profit in every property that you work on. By using these rings in conjunction with each other, you will come out a winner not only with the property but in the eyes of your partners as well.

BONUS CHAPTER 3

ADVANCED IRA INVESTMENT STRATEGIES

How would you like to earn hundreds of thousands of dollars TAX DEFERRED? Think about this—what if you could take $50,000 from your IRA—invest it in a great apartment property—and have it return to you $160,000 of profits WITHIN MONTHS all tax deferred? Earlier in the book, you saw me make mention that you can invest your IRA monies using my system into great Heartland of America apartment properties.

What I am going to cover in this chapter is how to do exactly that. Invest your IRA, Roth IRA, 401K and/or Keogh account into large tax deferred profits for your retirement.

Here is the nice thing about this.

Most people will go the USUAL route of investing their retirement accounts into a mutual fund and just let it ride the course, maybe contributing to the account month after month up to the limits imposed by the IRS. I think you would agree this is what most people do with their IRA accounts. Problem with this method is, it takes a long time, even tax deferred, to get large account balances built up doesn't it? For example, if I start out with an account balance of say $10,000 and add say $250 per month to that account it will take me approximately two to three years to get to an account balance of $20,000 AND that is if the market is good and positive each and every year, but it could be longer. Contrast that with our apartment property investing system and you can have that $10,000 into $20,000—with no monthly investing in about 9–12 months. How about that?

Let's use some bigger numbers that will really get you excited. Let's say I have $200,000 in my account and I add $4,000 per year. If all goes well I could have that account balance at around $300,000 in about 5 to 7 years and that is with a nice gain on the account balance every month. Again, contrast that with putting that same $200,000 into a nice apartment property and having it return $300,000 in about 18 months! Can you see how using your IRA money can, as I said in the beginning of the book, fold time back to our advantage??

The good news is, you don't have to use your entire IRA account and put it all into real estate. You can just transfer some into our apartment investment system and leave the rest in a more conservative investment.

Can you see how and why many of my partners and apartment investment clients do this??

Yeah, This Sounds Great But How Hard Is It? It Sounds Very Difficult and Technical.

Here is the good news. It is extremely easy to do! Let me give you the simple to follow steps of doing this. Keep in mind that I will be using IRA to also mean 401K, Roth IRA and Keogh as well since this applies to those investment vehicles as well. It prevents me from stating this every time....

1. Transfer your IRA account to a provider of Self-Directed IRA's. All you need do is get in touch with the companies that provide self directed IRA services and they will do most of the heavy lifting for you. (I have a list of such companies in the back of this chapter with some recommendations for you). What happens here is that you fill out paperwork that essentially transfers your IRA from the company you are with to a new company—one that lets you Self Direct (mean invest your IRA in what you want not what the company wants) your IRA monies. This paperwork goes to your new Self Directed company that goes through the process of transferring the money from your account into a new IRA account that gives you the power to invest in whatever you want and into what the law will allow.

For example. Lets say you have $200,000 in an IRA account with Fidelity Investments. You want to invest at least a part of this balance into a great apartment property using our apartment investment system. You simply contact a brokerage and investment company similar to Fidelity that provides Self Directed Investment of your IRA. Once you contact this company, they will send you the appropriate paperwork to fill out to transfer your IRA from Fidelity to your new Self Directed home. Once this paperwork is filled out and sent back to this company, they contact Fidelity who will transfer your IRA money over to them. Remember, your IRA is STILL an IRA—this is not a distribution ONLY a transfer from one company to another. Once the transfer takes place then you are free to invest your IRA into Apartments using this system. Time this takes? Usually 2 to 4 weeks.

2. Once your IRA is with the new company put it in a money market fund until you find a great project to invest in. You want to transfer your money now and have it available for a great deal NOT wait until you have a great deal and then transfer the money. You want to be able to react fast when a good project comes up. Keeping it in a money market fund at your NEW company will give you flexibility and you will not lose principal by investing in stocks or other mutual funds. Remember, most of these Self Directed IRA companies provide the same investments as the others like bonds, mutual funds, stocks, etc. but we want our money to be liquid and not lose principal. Of course if you want to place a portion of your IRA into another investment that is okay.

3. Find an apartment investment to put at least some of your IRA monies into. Now you are on the lookout for that apartment property investment using the system outlined in this book, and it is time to find the apartment investment. Again, make sure you follow the system and do not get impatient! This is your retirement money we are talking about here.

4. Once you have found the apartment property you want to invest in contact your Self Directed company to assist you with this.

Again, this is really simple and just a paperwork exercise. The Self Directed IRA company will forward you the appropriate paperwork (or have you complete it online) so that they can process the investment for you. Again, it is very easy.

5. Once you have invested in the apartment property, wait for those tax deferred profits to come back into your retirement account.

That's it! Could it be any easier??

Now really, I am not snow balling you. This is easy to do and many of my partners and clients do this everyday with amounts ranging from $5,000 - $5,000,000!

With that said however, there ARE some things you need to know and need to avoid. Make sure you take your time and read these items because if you make a mistake with your account, you could be liable for taxes on the balance and I know that you do not want to do that. So, here are the things to remember...

1. If the apartment property you are investing your IRA into requires financing, which most do, make sure you do NOT sign a personal guarantee. A personal guarantee is a document that the lender has you sign that says, in the event the bank would ever have to foreclose and sell the property AND not get enough in sales proceeds to cover the outstanding loan, then, they could go after you for whatever they are still owed. Do NOT sign this document. The IRS will consider this a withdrawal from your IRA since it is essentially being used as collateral for the personal guarantee. Remember, even if you are buying the apartment as a member of an LLC or using your own LLC the banks will many times STILL want you to sign a personal guarantee.

A good idea here is to give the lenders a heads up that you are going to be investing in an apartment project in the near future AND you may be using SOME IRA money to do that and that the IRS prohibits you from signing a personal guarantee. Ask the lender under what circumstances would they allow you to avoid signing a personal guarantee? This is important to do NOW because there are some lenders who will NOT budge from this and WILL want a personal guarantee signed, no matter what. If they will not budge from this then cross them off your short list for now. Bottom line? No personal guarantee!

2. Do Not Invest in a Risky Property. I know this is common sense but sometimes you will run into a property that doesn't feel right BUT the potential profits can be huge but there is a lot of risk. Avoid this high risk projects as much as possible.

3. Avoid properties where you may be subject to frequent capital calls. Make sure that the apartment project you are investing in is well funded so capital calls will not be necessary. A capital call is when you run out of money to run the property, finish the repair and maintenance items, etc. and the owners need to contribute out of their personal funds. With an IRA invested the capital that would be contributed would come from your IRA. Sometimes this is okay and not a problem, as long as it is rare and does not require a lot of money. Tip: make sure there are plenty of funds in reserve to cover any unforseen expenses BEFORE closing off the property. Most of the properties I own with partners have a large deposit of reserve funds to avoid capital calls.

4. Make sure any cash flows or profits from the property go back into your IRA account. Don't make the mistake of getting those cash flow or profit checks and cashing the checks yourself. No sir. Remember, this is IRA money and all profits need to go back into the IRA account. As a matter of fact all of the cash flow or profit checks need to be made out to your IRA, NOT to you.

5. Make sure your Self Directed IRA Company gets quarterly reports detailing the value of your IRA into the apartment property. For example, let's say you invest $200,000 into an apartment property in December. The following March you need to get an idea as to how much your $200,000 has grown and report this amount to your Self Directed IRA company. Same in June, September and December.

6. Make sure you do NOT take title to the property using your IRA—use an LLC. For example I would never want to take title to a property using Darin Garman, IRA because in the event there was a claim against me my IRA monies could be at risk. What you want to do is use an LLC to take title to a property and simply have your IRA as a member of that LLC. Again, I can form an LLC and call it Darin Garman, LLC and the member of that LLC can be my IRA. This gives you a layer of protection that you more than likely would never need, but, is cheap insurance against any possible problems.

7. Keep track of all monthly property operations and ask for property reports. You want to be kept up with what is going on so the best way to do this is to ask for monthly reports on the property. This will give you even more peace of mind.

IRA, KEOGH, ROTH IRA, 401 K investing into apartments is relatively easy to do. My company assists people with this all the time, and most invest in our projects here in the Heartland. I do have an IRA KIT that you will find helpful that you can download. Simply go to www.9monthinvestment.com and click on the IRA Kit link to download your information.

Hundreds of thousand in profits tax deferred! What else could get better?

Self Directed IRA Companies To Contact With My Preferences First:

Equity Trust Company
225 Burns Rd.
Elyria, OH 44035
Phone: 877-693-8206
Fax: 440-366-3750
www.trustetc.com

Guidant Financial
13122 NE 20th St.
Suite 100
Bellevue, WA 98005
Phone: 888-472-4455
www.guidantfinancial.com

Bonus Step–Use your IRA, SEP and/or KEOGH dollars to earn large profits TAX DEFERRED! You can get your IRA kit at www.9monthinvestment.com.

Bonus Chapter 4

Make Sure In Everything You Do in The World of Real Estate You Use The Take Away!

When you are looking for a Private Lender, you must act as if you do not need them at all. You must act as if it is THEM that will be missing out on a great project, a great return on their money and a great experience NOT the other way around.

You see, most people go about this backward. They approach with a posture of NEED. You know what I am talking about. We have all been approached from a posture of need. When you approach someone from a posture of need you are not much different from the vagrant approaching you asking you for money. How turned off are you by that? Frankly, not much difference between the guy begging you for money and you begging your relationships or prospects to join you. Always remember that when you approach someone from a posture of need, that you build an automatic wall of skepticism between you and the person you want money from and now you have to work hard, very hard to tear down that wall so that they at least SINCERELY consider it. Believe me, this is a tough row to hoe.

So, how should you approach someone? What should you do, say? How do they know what you have to "offer" if you do not approach someone for goodness sake and ask them for the money, for the investment, for the partnership??

First, the prerequisite is always approaching with an air of 'you could care less if they take advantage of this opportunity' and you are in a way giving them a break on letting them know about the project you are working on. Of course you do not say this to them but this is how your mindset needs to be. I will explain in a bit why it works much better this way (vs. begging) but for now, this is your mental approach— almost casual about them being involved with you or not. If they do they do, if they don't so what. This is your attitude.

Second, you need to mention what you are doing in passing in order to get them to ask YOU the questions about the deal. Read that last sentence again—you want them asking YOU about it. You want to throw triggers out there so they will ask YOU more questions. Let me give you a couple of examples:

You are out at the ballpark watching your kid play in a baseball game and you are sitting with a group of parents. You are talking to one of the parents about what everyone is doing this week, this weekend, etc. So, someone says to you, "Hey Bill, what do YOU have going on this weekend?" or the question can be 100 variations of this but you know what I am talking about. "How is it going?" "What have you been up to?", Etc. You say, "Well I have to spend some time on this real estate project that I am putting a partnership together to purchase." Let me ask you... Do you think you will now get 400 questions about this? You darn right you will. Now, remember you want to act is if this is an exclusive deal BUT you want to tease them with the HOT BUTTONS of the project when they follow up with more questions to you on this and believe me...they will.

Second Example:

Using a social networking site or blog that you may have to let people know what you are up to, again, without begging is a great idea. To be 'casually' mentioning how you are up to your neck with the latest real estate partnership you are putting together and that has kept you away from keeping your friends up to date with what you are doing is a smart move. Again, this kind of stuff will lead to questions FROM THEM, which gives you permission to tell them about the project you are working on. In relation to this, what helped me a lot early on, when the social networking sites were not all the rage, was to start my email responses with "sorry, been working on a complicated real estate project, and it has kept me away from my email", got me a lot of response and a lot of questions and eventually, some people joining me in the next commercial real estate project that I found.

Before I go any further I want to tell you why the approach of "take away selling" works. What is it that most people want? I mean, when it comes to what most people want you can be sure of one thing. It is something that they cannot have. You know what I mean? You typically, right now, want something that you can't have or don't have at the present. Even when you get the things that you want many times, you start looking for the next thing that you don't have don't you??

The same goes for our investments. We want to give people the feeling that this is something that they can't have and only a select few can. This is pretty close to the opposite of what most people do—they go right for the close and in many cases push and push for people to get involved in a DEAL with them. You do NOT want to do things this way—you want to almost take it away from them and get them to chase you! Believe me—this works!

The more you keep talking about a project that 'others' have been getting involved in with you and keep rubbing it in their noses that they have NOT done so, the more you will get people coming to you for this deal or for a future deal—leaving you basically with predisposed people wanting in on your next real estate project.

Do you see the change in psychology here? When are you in a stronger position? When you are calling those or talking to those around you cold on a deal that you are desperate to get done OR you have THEM CALLING YOU or APPROACHING YOU about it? You know the answer.

I discovered this on my first large project by accident. This project required about $1,500,000 to get it done and I was of course scrambling to get the funding. It was going slow. Then, I started to change my approach and my marketing a bit. I started to tell people how this deal compared with past deals that went very well. I talked about the hot button points as you might imagine—cash flow, return, faster wealth building, etc. What I did NOT do was pitch the property—I only talked about how good it was compared to what others got involved in with me in the past. If they happened to want information on it I gave them a means to get some information from me on the project. Again, no hard sell.

Once they requested the information, I told them that based on how well this project was going to do as compared with the past properties and the interest that I had in it so far, I would not be surprised if it was fully funded very soon. I then left them my contact information in the event of questions or clarifications. Again, no hard sell.

I will be damned if this approach drove people into a competition with others and we were fully funded on this within a matter of a few days! I had people bending over backwards to get in touch with me so they would not miss out on this project.

If you have ever looked at my marketing or have talked to me personally I have never really pushed the hard sell—I have always given the impression that if you do it, great, if not—your loss! In my opinion that is the position you want to me in most of the time. This is the real position of strength!

So keep this in mind. You will be tempted to really push your deal and hard sell it and there will be instances where this is OK—however you want to use takeaway selling as much as possible—because—it will work.

I have a "Basics of Take Away Selling In Real Estate" report on my web site at www.9monthinvestment.com which will help you tremendously. Make sure you get there.

I think you get the idea of this chapter but let's sum it up anyway. When you use your relationships as leverage to get private money, you do it in a way that makes THEM ask you the questions about what it is you are doing and you ACT AS IF you could care less if they were to ever get involved but you keep answering their questions and sharing information with them if they ask or request it. You want to really sell them on the idea that this is an EXCLUSIVE DEAL and that it is only privy to a chosen few. Once they get that feeling they will be putty in your hands because THEY will want in on it as well.

What you can expect out of doing this an ongoing curiosity about what you are doing that will eventually lead to business for you from some of these folks. Most will not do anything of course but for them to know what you are up to in a non threatening way will get talked about and circulated among people and you will have people getting in touch with you just from this word of mouth.

Bonus Chapter 5

Hassle Free Management To Fast Profits

Good news! You finally closed on your apartment property purchase! You made money at the closing table and now its time to get to work and realize that profit as soon as possible!

But now comes the hard part. Now you have to take this property from where it is now to where you know it can be in terms of value and cash flow. You have followed all of our litmus tests and you have used the rule of 9% to lock in those profits. Now is the time to get the property to its ultimate value and profit.

With that in mind I want to share with you how you can do this with little hassle and time out of your day. That is correct, I will show you how you can do this and never have to deal with a tenant if you don't want to.

First, You Start By Making the Decision That You Will Not Be A Manager Of The Property and Be Emotionally Okay With That. For some, this will be an easy decision, for others it may be difficult because you want to make sure everything is done right and if you want it done right, you need to do it yourself.

Remember, this book is about how to simplify your wealth goals and not how to make them more complicated. The last thing you need to be doing is showing units to tenants, taking rental applications or fixing the stopped up sink.

This of course goes to Murphy's Law #22 which states that any time a problem happens at a rental property and would need your attention as the owner and manager will be when you are:

1. On vacation.
2. Going on vacation.
3. At an important function.
4. At night.
5. On a weekend.
6. Always at the worst possible time.

So look, if you want to be a good property manager go into the property management business. For what we want to accomplish lets leave the heavy lifting to the experts Okay?

This gets down to not getting yourself in the trap of doing it yourself because if you want the job done right, well, you HAVE to do it yourself.

NO! Don't do that!

The management structure that you will put into place is not going to be perfect. The management company employees will do things differently than you would, they will talk differently than you would and they may treat the tenants differently that you would and hey, they may even do the bookkeeping differently than you would. So what! Make sure that your attitude about this is to let the professionals do the day-to-day management while you do the profit management!

You are going to be hiring the professionals to do this for you and you cannot be coaching from the sidelines. However, there ARE some expectations that you will want from you management company and I will get into that in a little bit.

So first, stay out of the management companies way and let them do their jobs.

Getting Your Property Management Company In Place.

In previous chapters I take you through the litmus test of choosing a property management company for your project. Make sure you follow that advice and you will be set and will be off and running right after your closing.

However, there are some things we need to do before the management company storms the beaches of your property. Here they are:

1. Have a meeting with the managers about two weeks before closing. You should already have had a meeting with the management company before this time but now is the time to plot a strategy for the property and to make sure the management company knows of your expectations. Also, this will be a good time for you to go over what the management company is going to be getting into with this property in terms of vacancies, possible repairs, tenant issues, etc. This is the time where you tell the property management folks that the goal is to make this property as profitable as possible as quickly as possible by doing the following:

    A) Getting Rents Up To Market Levels of All Currently Occupied and Vacant units. This is where you turn the management company loose on getting the rents that the property should have been getting months or in some cases years ago. Not only do you want the management company to be renting any vacant units for the market rents you want to get those units that are currently being rented up to market level ASAP! Now, depending on how much longer these tenants have on their leases you may be able to do this within 30 days OR you may have to wait a few months. Point being you cannot raise a tenants rent until their lease expires. So, you want the managers to be letting these tenants know that their rents will be going up about 35–40 days prior to their leases expiring.

B) Working On Increasing Not Only Rents But Additional Income Sources. Does the laundry need to go up 50 cents to one dollar or more for each load? Do you need to be charging for use of the garages instead of letting the tenants use them for free? Can you start leasing out closet space for $10.00 per month, etc. Now is the time you sit down with your management folks and talk about other ways that the income from the property will be increased!

C) Working on Repair, Maintenance and Cosmetic Repair Items. This is where you lay out a schedule as to what needs to be done and when. For example do the common areas need painting? Do the common area carpets need to be changed? Are there any vacant units that need to have new carpet, paint and be freshened up? Do any of the mechanical systems need to be checked and made ready for the summer and or winter? Right here is where you give the management team a schedule of what kind of work you feel needs to be done AND A DEADLINE FOR THE COMPLETION OF THAT WORK! Make sure you go over deadlines with them and make sure you are both on the same page in terms of whether these items can be achieved by the date you expect and if not when.

D) Working on Decreasing Your Expenses. Remember just like the income rule of 9% we now have to start working on the expense reduction of 9% and your management folks can be a huge help here but keep in mind that you will have to do most of the work here. Most management companies are good at babysitting things like garbage collection, lawn mowing, snow removal, etc. but they do not necessarily know the best vendor at the lowest cost. Make sure that when it comes to lowering your property taxes, property insurance costs, lawn and snow, utilities, etc. that you do your homework on this first but be prepared for recommendations from your management company. You do NOT have to use who they recommend but they may know something you don't. Whatever you do, do not leave it up to the management company to use vendors unless you approve of them by the job they do and the cost. Again, the big expense reduction items like property tax reduction, insurance premium reduction, etc. will more than likely fall in your lap—plan on it. For the other items have the management company get you three bids on everything then decide who to use based on using the rule of 9%.

E) Working On Getting As Many Unoccupied Units Occupied As Soon As Possible. I will talk more about this in my next point but once a unit is fresh and ready to go there should be no excuse as to why it is not rented as of yet. It should only take a couple of weeks at the most to get a unit filled with a good tenant. If the leasing agents for the management company are doing their job this should be pretty easy—especially with the amount of activity that has been going on around the property.

F) Keeping and Attracting the Right Tenant To Your Property—The Most Important Item. When it comes down to having the property that will increase in value the most you have learned by now that it is pretty much all about the numbers. That is about 90% of it. It's the numbers that an investor or bank will buy into once you decide to sell for a profit or possibly refinance, pull cash out and do it again.

But, there is 10% that is very important too. That 10% is the type of tenant that lives in your apartments and is allowed to live in your apartments in the first place. I cannot stress to you enough how important it is to fill your apartments with (and keep current) tenants that are GOOD TENANTS! What do I mean by a GOOD TENANT? Here is my criteria:

1. They have a job.
2. They are consistently at work.

3. They take pride in their appearance and their vehicles.
4. They have a checking account and a savings account.
5. They have good credit—not GREAT—but good.
6. They take pride in the way their apartment will look.
7. They have an excellent payment history with former landlords.
8. Bottom line? THEY ARE RESPONSIBLE!

That is right, you are looking for responsible people to live in your units. Responsible people attract responsible people. This is what you want, not only to give you good cash flow and less management hassle but huge gains in resale. Let me ask you—would you pay more for a property where the management was tough and the tenants were tough to deal with? Of course not! It's about resale!!

Speaking of this, here is the type of tenants you should avoid and make sure this is communicated to your property managers:

1. Unemployed or on a small disability payment.
2. Mentally ill adults.
3. Large families of unemployed people that will hang out most of the day.
4. Low or no income.
5. People that are sloppy, dirty in their appearance and their vehicles appearance.
6. People on housing assistance.
7. People with large pets.
8. People that are NOT RESPONSIBLE.

Now of course your management company cannot discriminate based on color, religion, etc. but make sure you take a good look at this list since this is where 99% of your problems will be. It is hard to jump a property in value when you have tenants that will cause headaches, collection and maintenance and repair problems.

You want to make sure; you and your management company are on the same page with this. For example if the property had a bunch of people that were low life drug users you don't want the management company to think that keeping these kinds of folks around in your building is going to be acceptable. Time to lay down the law.

The good news is once you have this conversation with your management company, they will get it and should do a good job for you—BUT—make sure you have the conversation.

FREE

An Invitation From Darin Garman To Get Your Hands On The 9 Month Investment Tool Kit! Complete With Easy To Follow Tools And Resources To Explode Your Wealth RIGHT NOW Instead of Waiting Years!

You can have the same resources in your hands TODAY that have been used by me for years. Talk about a shortcut! You can get your hands on the 9 Month Tool Kit By:

Web: www.9monthinvestment.com/toolkit

Mail This Page: 9 Month Investment Tool Kit
743 10th St.
Marion, Iowa 52302

FAX This Page: 1-866-212-2838

Fill This Out!

Name:_____

Address:_____

City:_____

State:_____ Zip:_____

Email: _____

BUY A SHARE OF THE FUTURE IN YOUR COMMUNITY

These certificates make great holiday, graduation and birthday gifts that can be personalized with the recipient's name. The cost of one S.H.A.R.E. or one square foot is $54.17. The personalized certificate is suitable for framing and will state the number of shares purchased and the amount of each share, as well as the recipient's name. The home that you participate in "building" will last for many years and will continue to grow in value.

Here is a sample SHARE certificate:

YES, I WOULD LIKE TO HELP!

I support the work that Habitat for Humanity does and I want to be part of the excitement! As a donor, I will receive periodic updates on your construction activities but, more importantly, I know my gift will help a family in our community realize the dream of homeownership. **I would like to SHARE in your efforts against substandard housing in my community!** *(Please print below)*

PLEASE SEND ME _____ SHARES at $54.17 EACH = $ $_____

In Honor Of: _____

Occasion: (Circle One)   HOLIDAY   BIRTHDAY   ANNIVERSARY

     OTHER: _____

Address of Recipient: _____

Gift From: _____ *Donor Address:* _____

Donor Email: _____

I AM ENCLOSING A CHECK FOR $ $_____ PAYABLE TO HABITAT FOR HUMANITY <u>OR</u> PLEASE CHARGE MY VISA OR MASTERCARD *(CIRCLE ONE)*

Card Number _____ Expiration Date: _____

Name as it appears on Credit Card _____ Charge Amount $ _____

Signature _____

Billing Address _____

Telephone # Day _____ Eve _____

PLEASE NOTE: Your contribution is tax-deductible to the fullest extent allowed by law.
Habitat for Humanity • P.O. Box 1443 • Newport News, VA 23601 • 757-596-5553
www.HelpHabitatforHumanity.org